# *Grace*
*in the*
# *Wilderness*

*Reflections on God's Sustaining Word*
*Along Life's Journey*

Cover and book design by Mary E. Bolin.
Photographs by Br. Francis Wagner, O.S.B.

Reflections adapted from www.yokeofchrist.blogspot.com
and www.pathoflifeblog.blogspot.com.

ISBN 978-0-87029-552-2
Library of Congress 2013919762

Published by Abbey Press
1 Hill Drive   St. Meinrad, IN 47577
Printed by Abbey Press in United States of America.
www.pathoflifebooks.com

# *Grace* in the *Wilderness*

## Reflections on God's Sustaining Word Along Life's Journey

*by Br. Francis de Sales Wagner, O.S.B.*

Path of Life Publications
*Spiritual Food for the Christian Journey* from **Abbey Press**

# Contents

# God in the Moment

# Christian Life

# Faith

# Hope

# Love

# Peace and Joy

# Redemption and Resurrection

"Thus says the Lord: The people who survived the sword found grace in the wilderness; when my people sought for rest, the Lord appeared to them from far away. I will turn their mourning into joy. I will comfort them, and give them gladness for sorrow. Keep your voice from weeping, and your eyes from tears; there is hope for your future, says the Lord. Set up road markers for yourself, make yourself guideposts; consider well the highway, the road by which you went. Return, my beloved; return to the Lord your God. I will make a new covenant with my people. I will put my law within them, and I will write it on their hearts; and I will be their God, and they shall be my people. They shall all know me, from the least of them to the greatest, says the Lord; for I will forgive their iniquity, and remember their sin no more."

—Jeremiah 31

# Introduction

Y ou are not alone. Whatever the circumstances may be and no matter how you may feel at any given moment, no matter what you may have done or failed to do, no matter how painful or hopeless things may seem, one thing is certain: God is with you. There *is* hope for your future.

This is the promise of God's Word to us. Wherever we may be physically, emotionally, and especially spiritually, God is prepared to meet us, journey with us, and lead us out of the wilderness. The route may not be the one we would have chosen for ourselves, but grace ultimately guides us toward joy, gladness, purpose, reconciliation, and redemption beyond anything we can imagine. Crooked lines are made straight. Along the way, we need only to put our faith in the voice that softly whispers in our hearts, as it was proclaimed to a dispirited people by the prophet Haggai: "Take courage, all you people, says the Lord. I am with you. My spirit abides among you; do not fear" (Haggai 2:4-5).

This is grace in the wilderness, as the prophet Jeremiah wrote so long ago to give the exiled Israelites hope, evoking the memory of an even earlier time when God led their ancestors out of slavery in Egypt. It is essentially the same message of hope and transformation declared by all the prophets, and ultimately fulfilled in Jesus Christ, the Word made flesh:

> who, though he was in the form of God,
>     did not regard equality with God
>     as something to be exploited,
> but emptied himself,
>     taking the form of a slave,
>     being born in human likeness.

*And being found in human form,*
   *he humbled himself*
   *and became obedient to the point of death—*
   *even death on a cross.*
                              —Philippians 2:6-8

This magnificent manifestation of God's love for us—for *you*—is the point of Scripture, with Christ's resurrection and ascension, and the outpouring of the Holy Spirit at Pentecost providing the exclamation point.

The reflections in this book simply retell this story or forward the message—hopefully, in faithful and prayerful fashion. Unfortunately (sometimes tragically), Scripture is often reduced to a moral code of conduct, a narrow-minded justification for various causes, or a blanket of sentimentality with which we insulate ourselves. But life is messier than that. I know that; you know that; God knows that. Inspired by God, the Bible was written by human beings who lived, struggled, and died amid the same perplexities and contradictions in life in which we find ourselves today. Modernity only gives them a new face. In one way or another, and at one time or another, we are each lost and need to be found. We wander in the wilderness, attempting to survive the various "swords" that are thrust our way. In our willful independence and disobedience, we turn this way and that (sometimes thrusting our own swords!). We seek—through various things, behaviors, or relationships—the rest that only God can provide. We seem to be abandoned. We mourn and sorrow. We weep, and our eyes are filled with tears.

Where is God? Right *there*—not up in the clouds or in some vague event too distant to consider; not in a false sense of security or certainty. Paradoxically, we find grace *in* the wilderness—redemption in the crucifixion. "The mysteries of Christ are our mysteries," as Blessed Columba Marmion said. With the eyes of faith, we can see (albeit dimly) God's sustaining presence in the *midst* of all that would seem to deny it. The late 19th- and early 20th-century French poet and dramatist Paul Claudel sums it up nicely: "Jesus did not come to remove suffering, or to explain it, but to fill it with his presence."

God does not cause suffering or justify the human malfeasance that ultimately gives rise to it. In the person of Christ, the Good

2

Shepherd, he comes to redeem what was lost and release what was imprisoned. He comes to rebuild what was destroyed, to reunite what was scattered, and to regenerate what had seemed lifeless. "Indeed, God did not send the Son into the world to condemn the world, but in order that the world might be saved through him" (John 3:17).

In other words, your life at *this very moment* has meaning—if you allow that meaning to unfold within it, that grace to take root in the wilderness.

Viewed as a whole, this is the promise of Scripture, and the good news I hope to convey through the collection of meditations in this book. The fruit of my own prayer, study, and reflection, they are primarily gathered from posts on my personal blog (first, *yoke-ofchrist.blogspot.com*, and, later, *pathoflifeblog.blogspot.com*) from 2009 to 2013. Although most were written with a view toward the liturgical year in the Roman Catholic Church and its cycle of readings for Mass, they have been adapted and arranged thematically here under the general sections: Grace, Prayer, The Body of Christ, Conversion, God in the Moment, Christian Life, Faith, Hope, Love, Peace and Joy, and Redemption and Resurrection. (For those interested in reading the reflections in accordance with their original placement within the liturgical cycle of readings, an index is provided at the end of the book; it must be noted, however, that not *every* entry has such a placement.)

Given their original context, then, these reflections clearly do not represent some attempt at a systematic, scholarly examination of either Scripture or the nature of grace. Each meditation was written as an individual piece at a certain point in time. It so happens (after I finally heeded blog readers who urged me to collect the posts into a book), that when they were gathered, adapted, and organized thematically, together the reflections seemed to coalesce around the theme outlined above. If that is true—you can be the judge—then, perhaps, that *itself* is grace. Somehow, God finds a way to repeatedly sound the message—even through flawed instruments such as myself.

Most of the book's reflections are intently focused on Scripture, with numerous references throughout to relevant passages. Readers, then, are invited to use a Bible in conjunction with this book and meditate on the cited texts themselves. Hopefully, the reflections stand on their own, but I think each will resonate more clearly if one takes the time to read the corresponding passages from Scripture. Ultimately, I pray that this book is one you can pick up anytime to help facilitate your reflection on Scripture and its relation to your own life, so that you may experience God's grace in the wilderness.

One final logistical note: Throughout this book, I refer quite often to New Testament passages with phrases such as "St. Paul wrote," or "as St. Paul said"—even in cases where modern scholarship has reasonably questioned whether the texts are *directly* from Paul's hand. This is done for the sake of simplicity and because such letters are recognized—at the least—as "Pauline" in the sense of developing his ideas. Rather than confuse the issue, I refer to the letters' author in the traditional manner.

St. Paul, of course, is perhaps the world's most renowned beneficiary of grace, as he himself realized: "I am the least of the apostles, unfit to be called an apostle, because I persecuted the church of God," he writes in the First Letter to the Corinthians (15:19-20). "But by the grace of God I am what I am, and his grace toward me has not been in vain. On the contrary, I worked harder than any of them—though it was not I, but the grace of God that is with me." His conversion from persecutor to apostle led to the rapid spread of Christianity in a way that could not have been foreseen. While this work was immensely fruitful, it was far from easy.

Whatever trials and obstacles he encountered in the wilderness of his own life (cf. 2 Corinthians 11:23-30), Paul seemed to have an intuitive sense of what grace is and what it means. "I have been crucified with Christ," he wrote to the Galatians (2:19-20). "It is no longer I who live, but it is Christ who lives in me. And the life I now live in the flesh I live by faith in the Son of God, who loved me and gave himself for me."

Grace is God's very presence among us and within us, in the midst of all that would seem to argue against it. Jeremiah sought to bolster the hope of the Israelites after the fall of Jerusalem and their exile to Babylon in 587 B.C. Their Temple destroyed and their homeland taken from them, they seemed to have lost absolutely everything as captives in a foreign land. The prophet's statement, writes Old Testament scholar Walter Brueggemann in his *Commentary on Jeremiah,* "makes an allusion back to the wilderness sojourn in the ancient days of Moses, when God surprisingly gave sustenance in the wilderness (cf. Exodus 16:12; Jeremiah 2:2). At the same time, however, 'wilderness' is a reference to contemporary exile, so that the assertion not only remembers surprising graciousness in the past, but is a statement concerning God's powerful, gracious presence" in present circumstances. "The present reality of exile is not godless and not graceless."

The same is no less true for each one of us today. Just as with the ancient Israelites, God walks in our midst through the wilderness, and beckons us to follow. Just as the pillars of cloud and fire signifying God's presence went ahead of Moses and his people as they journeyed out of Egypt (Exodus 13:17-22); just as the cloud filled Solomon's newly built Temple in Jerusalem (1 Kings 8:10-13); and just as the heavens parted over Jesus at his baptism to reveal the Spirit of God and the Father's declaration, "This is my Son, the Beloved" (Matthew 3:16-17)—God is with us every inch of the way. And just as Jesus—*Emmanuel,* "God is with us (cf. Matthew 1:23)—is led by the Spirit into the wilderness to face trial and temptation (Matthew 4:1-11; Mark 1:12-13; Luke 4:1-13), so are we. But we are not alone; God *joins us* in that struggle, as the wonderful mystery of the Incarnation demonstrates. God voluntarily limits himself in human form to re-establish a partnership of grace with all of creation, thereby providing hope for our future.

The same Spirit which Jesus breathed upon his disciples (cf. John 20:21-22) is conferred upon us at Baptism. This Holy Spirit now animates the Body of Christ, the Church—through the very human (and still-flawed) life of its members, through worship and the Sacraments, and through Scripture, God's Word to us. Through these means, in God "we live and move and have our being" (Acts 17:28). They provide us with the strength and courage we need to persevere, and the vision to see beyond the seeming barrenness of present circumstances toward the promise that all things are made new in Christ. They guide our course toward joy, gladness, purpose, reconciliation, and redemption. They give us the grace of God—who reveals himself in the wilderness. ♣

Grace

# Grace in the Wilderness

**H**ave faith. We hear that statement often enough, but what does it really *mean*?

In the Book of the Prophet Jeremiah (31:1-7), God promises to restore and rebuild the kingdom of the ancient Hebrews after their division, conquest, and exile. God pledges to deliver them from captivity and make them joyful and fruitful again, united in their own land. As we know, God kept that promise. Still, the period of difficulty that the Israelites endured served a purpose—it led them to turn their hearts toward God, to pray for deliverance with trust in God's providence with humility and perseverance. That's faith—and the exile experience helped sharpen its focus.

Jeremiah alludes to the experience of the exiles' ancestors, who were led by Moses out of slavery in Egypt toward the Promised Land. They spent 40 years journeying through the desert, an experience God used to test and sharpen their faith. Ultimately, it is Jesus—the new Moses—who fulfills the promise of deliverance and entry into the Promised Land of the Heavenly Kingdom.

United with Christ, we too have our deserts to cross, our exile experiences to endure, therefore providing the opportunity for faith to be tested and purified. As you will recall, before he began his ministry, Jesus was led by the Spirit into the desert for 40 days to be tempted by Satan. He persevered, sustained by the Father who sent him.

It's not something we like to hear, but Scripture's consistent message is that our fallen human condition necessarily involves hardship, failure, and suffering. And yet, there is something about such universal experiences that prompt us to cry out to God in a way we would be likely to rarely consider if life were always a bed of roses. The good news is that God joins us in the briar patch, so to speak, to lead us out. Yes, he could remove the briar patch from our path altogether, but he won't. To do that, he would have to over-ride humanity's greatest God-given attribute—the free will which we, as a race, so often misdirect, creating the conditions under which so many suffer. Instead, in the Second Person of the Holy Trinity, God takes on our human flesh, allows himself to be pierced by the very same thorns that wound us, and says, "Follow me. I am with you always." In this way, the very effects of sin are transformed by God into the means of redemption.

Along the way, he provides something we cannot see or feel—the grace that fuels faith, trust, humility, and perseverance. When we turn to God in the midst of our own exiles and desert journeys, we discover, as St. Paul says, that "I can do all things through him who strengthens me" (Philippians 4:13). Jeremiah tells us that the exiles "found grace in the wilderness" (31:2). In the wilderness of hardship, failure, and suffering, God's people find the grace to sustain them along the journey to the Promised Land.

How? Prayer. Simple, sincere, steadfast prayer. The story of the Canaanite woman provides the perfect example (Matthew 15:21-28). She cries out to Jesus with faith, trust, humility, and perseverance. She is straightforward, and she is persistent. Jesus not only grants her request, but praises this pagan woman for her faith—obviously meant as a "teaching moment" for the "chosen" people who failed to display such attributes. She prays, and is answered—not because of any merit, but because of her faith.

This is the "grace in the wilderness" of which Jeremiah speaks. May we all find such grace; it's ours for the asking, even if it's a simple, "Lord, help my unbelief" (cf. Mark 9:24). It is faith that saves, and the grace of prayer provides it. "For by grace you have been saved through faith, and this is not your own doing; it is the gift of God" (Ephesians 2:8).

Our prayer, then, must coincide with the very last sentence in the Bible: "The grace of the Lord Jesus be with all" (Revelation 22:21) who journey through the wilderness of this life. ❧

# The Bridge of Grace

A mistaken notion—even among devoted Christians—has persisted for centuries. In some small measure, at least, many of us give in to it. This is the idea that the Old Testament and the New Testament contradict one another, that the Old Covenant is about punishment, and the New Covenant is about mercy, and that Jesus came to do away with all that came before him. Somewhere along the line, it seems, God changed his mind about how to deal with us.

This short-sighted view overlooks what Jesus himself says very clearly: "Do not think that I have come to abolish the law or the prophets; I have come not to abolish but to fulfill" (Matthew 5:17).

God promised us a Redeemer from the very first moment after the Fall of our first parents (cf. Genesis 3:15). Jesus, the incarnate *Logos* (or Word) who reveals God the Father, pre-existed from the very beginning of creation, and through him all things came to be, as St. John tells us in the poetic opening lines of his Gospel (cf. John 1:1-5). In the Gospel of St. Luke (4:16-21), we are told that Jesus went to the synagogue in his hometown of Nazareth, where he was handed a scroll from the prophet Isaiah so that he could read a passage (cf. Isaiah 61:1-2; 58:6) to those present:

> "The Spirit of the Lord is upon me, because he has anointed me to bring good news to the poor. He has sent me to proclaim release to the captives and recovery of sight to the blind, to let the oppressed go free, to proclaim the year of the Lord's favor." And he rolled up the scroll, gave it back to the attendant, and sat down. The eyes of all

in the synagogue were fixed on him. Then he began to say to them, "Today, this scripture has been fulfilled in your hearing."

This shocked his listeners—his own townspeople—who responded by trying to throw him over a cliff! But, he was there in the flesh—Emmanuel, "God among us"—just as the prophets had foretold, to bridge the gap between old and new, and to demonstrate God's love for the poor, captive, blind, and oppressed—terms that describe *all of us*, both then and now, in one way or another. All of Scripture and Christian revelation is a unity, with Christ—fully human, fully divine—at the very center. All of it—Old Testament and New Testament—points to, or is fulfilled in, Christ. God is One (and, as we know, One in Three), and God is love (1 John 4:8, 16).

In Matthew's Gospel, Jesus draws on two Old Testament passages (Deuteronomy 6:4-5 and Leviticus 19:18) to summarize God's "greatest commandment": "You shall love the Lord your God with all your heart, and with all your soul, and with all your mind. This is the greatest and first commandment. And a second is like it: You shall love your neighbor as yourself. *On these two commandments hang all the law and the prophets.*"

And in St. John's Gospel, on the night before he died, Jesus tells his apostles (and us): "This is my commandment, that you *love one another as I have loved you*" (John 15:12).

Here is what St. Augustine has to say about all this:

Open the Bible at any page and you will find it extolling love. [The ancient peoples of the Old Testament] saw that all the precepts and promises of the old covenant, geared to the capacities of an unregenerate people, prefigured a new covenant, which the Lord would bring to fulfillment in the last age. The Apostle [Paul] says this quite clearly: *The things that happened to them were symbolic, and were recorded for us who are living in the last age.* When the time for it came, the new covenant began to be openly proclaimed, and those ancient figures were expounded and explained so that all might understand that the old covenant promises pointed to the new covenant.

And so love was present under the old covenant just as it is under the new, though then it was more hidden and fear was more apparent, whereas now love is more clearly seen and fear is diminished. For as love grows stronger we feel more secure, and when our feeling of security is complete, fear vanishes, since, as the apostle John declares: *Perfect love casts out fear* [1 John 4:18].

From this perspective, both the Old and New Testament are in perfect harmony with one another. What is revealed to us through both is this: human frailty (nature) gives way to divine power (grace)—with Christ as the bridge supporting our journey from one to the other.

Scripture must be read with a view toward the whole, in the light of Christ. And when we do this, we see that from the very beginning, the message has been clear, simple, and consistent, both in the Old Testament and in the New: *God loves us. We are to love God. We are to love ourselves as created by God. And we are to love others as God loves each one of us. Period.* That's it in a nutshell. And Christ—given to us in Word, Sacrament, and the living Tradition of the Church—is the One who makes it all possible from our end.

But we have to accept this Good News on the basis of faith *first*. Contrary to the world's wisdom, we must believe, and *then* see. And this doesn't mean everything will be crystal clear or easy as pie from that point onward. This is why we cry out along with the father of the disturbed child in Mark 9:24: "I believe; help my unbelief!" This is the most powerful confession of faith we can possibly utter. In it, humanity longs for the divine, nature longs for grace. And if we accept and respond to it, by divine grace we become what we desire.

"See," God tells us, "I am making all things new" (Revelation 21:5). ♣

# Security Gate

How can the shepherd also be a *gate*? Jesus claims to be both in the Gospel of John's well-known "Good Shepherd" discourse (John 10:1-10). The image of Jesus (and God) as shepherd has deep roots throughout Scripture and has provided comfort and assurance for many believers. However, a closer look at the passage reveals that the focus is on a *gate*. "I am the gate for the sheep," Jesus says. "Whoever enters by me will be saved, and will come in and go out and find pasture."

How are we to reconcile these two images? After all, Psalm 23 begins with the words, "The Lord is my *shepherd*," not, "The Lord is my *gate*."

Perhaps we interpret the word shepherd too narrowly—as someone who only guides, comforts, and provides for his flock. That is all certainly true. But a shepherd also protects, defends, and rescues the flock, even at the risk of his own life.

Recall that Christ is prefigured by David, a shepherd in his youth who, before going off to fight Goliath, pointed out to King Saul that he had slain lions and bears to save his father's sheep (1 Samuel 17:34-37). In a fuller way, Jesus does the same for us, the sheep of his pasture. He defeats the power of sin and death by giving up his own life so that we might "have life and have it abundantly" (John 10:10). By his wounds, we have been healed.

And there is this: In Jesus' time, the shepherd would protect his flock at night by herding the sheep into an enclosure with rock walls (a sheepfold, either circular or rectangular in shape). He would then position his own body across the single entrance to prevent the sheep from straying out into harm's way and to keep preying beasts and marauders out—unless they came through *him* first. He *became* the gate. In this way, the shepherd "laid down his life" for the sheep, just as Jesus does for us through the cross—our gateway to eternal life.

This is a striking image to consider. Jesus is our gateway to salvation and eternal life. He is shepherd and guardian, and through him we find pasture and repose for our souls. *Alleluia!* ♠

# Prayer

# Invitation to Prayer

A s Christians, we are all called to encounter and embrace God's Word to each of one of us—individually—deep within our hearts. Personal prayer is simply the means by which we train ourselves to be more aware of our relationship with God and his presence in the world.

The relationship already exists; personal prayer is what nourishes it.

By this, I do not mean to imply that public or liturgical prayer is unimportant. To the contrary, it is *essential*; public worship is how the Body of Christ expresses itself, transcends time, and joins eternity in the praise of God. It cannot be separated from personal prayer as if they were each distinct or competing aspects of faith. They are intimately bound with one another, just like breathing requires *both* inhaling *and* exhaling. They feed one another. Without one, the other dies.

But the focus here, for now, is on personal prayer—and more specifically, that silent surrender to God's movement of grace within our hearts.

Trappist monk Michael Casey, in his book *Toward God: The Ancient Wisdom of Western Prayer*, says:

> Prayer is an attempt to realize the love that unites us with God, allow it to become more present to us, and give it greater scope to act upon us and change us. We do not produce prayer. We allow prayer to act. We do not create prayer; it creates us.

In prayer, we listen for the invitation, for that "tiny whispering sound" in our hearts that draws us toward God. And to do this, we must surrender, let go of our preoccupations, our preconceived notions, our expectations, and simply be still before the God who created us, chose us, and redeemed us—the God who knows us better than we know ourselves. After all, "we live and move and have our being" (Acts 17:28) in God alone.

Each of us is a member of the Body of Christ, and we relate to the whole through each other. But each of us also has a personal and unique invitation from God. God's Word is sown in our *hearts*, and it is *there* that he calls us. We are born with this desire, or spiritual hunger, to seek God, but we must truly listen for the genuine invitation (among the myriad false and empty ones designed to distract us). We must be willing to follow Jesus into the dark and silent desert, and let him feed us with the bread from heaven.

"Ask and it will be given to you; search, and you will find; knock, and the door will be opened for you," Jesus tells us in the Gospel of Matthew (7:7-8), "Everyone who asks receives, and everyone who searches finds, and for everyone who knocks, the door will be opened."

We all do well to reflect on these words and on what they really mean. If we are willing to follow Jesus into the desert to be fed, to seek, to knock, to ask, just what is it we truly desire—deep down in our souls, which words cannot begin to express?

In the Gospel of Mark, Jesus asks a very simple question, one he poses to each and every one of us amid our busy lives, our work, our prayer, our failures, our successes, our joys, our sorrows:

*"What do you want me to do for you?"*

Actually, he asks the same question twice (see Mark 10:32-52). First, Jesus asks two of his apostles, James and John. They ask for power and glory. *Wrong answer.* Next, he asks a blind beggar by the road, who says, "Master, I want to see." In other words, "I want to see you, follow you." His was the correct answer because while he asked from his deepest need, his focus was on Jesus and not himself, nor his preconceived ideas and expectations.

*What do you want me to do for you?* It takes a hungry heart to answer that question truthfully. This scares many people because it means being vulnerable, acknowledging our need. We don't *like* to feel that way. We don't *want* to be hungry. We want to be full. But, too often, we fill ourselves with the wrong things and are left dissatisfied. Only the Bread of Life satisfies.

Personal prayer teaches us how to enter into the question. And it must be pure prayer from the heart, arising from that personal hunger—that *need*. It must be fiery prayer, beyond words, immersed in the love of God, as the ancient monk John Cassian would say.

This is contemplation, and we are all called to it. In heaven, we will spend an eternity doing it. Here, by God's grace, we are given a foretaste if we are open to it. It is not complicated, and it cannot be taught. It requires only a heart completely open to God's grace.

Christians—especially men—tend to over-intellectualize prayer and the spiritual life, to classify it, and systematize it. We make it something to be studied and taught, something to produce practical results like a good, moral life. That is all good and necessary. Our prayer *must* be informed, have structure, be communal, and make us better people. However, that is not all that true invitation to prayer involves. God did not become man merely to teach or introduce a system of moral conduct, or to inspire our involvement in a myriad of activities and programs. Jesus came to love us, to call us, to draw us, to invite us into his saving action of grace. We are called Christians not because of what we do, but because of who we are. "Come to me," Jesus says, to discover who you are truly meant to be.

In this invitation, God promises us his presence. "I am with you," he says repeatedly in Scripture. The gift of presence is the most valuable gift we can either receive or give. It is the gift of self. Prayer is simply being present to God, who is always present to us.

*"What do you want me to do for you? Ask and it will be given you."*

Whatever the answer to that question might be for you, God has accomplished it in Christ, and he reveals it through your personal hunger. Your deepest desire will be satisfied by your greatest need. ♣

# Hunger for God

Where do we encounter this personal hunger and find what truly fills us? As a pilgrim people belonging to God, we are called like the ancient Israelites into the desert—where it is dry, desolate, untamed, and uninhabited. God calls us where he can most fully manifest himself to us.

Spiritually speaking, the desert is where we have no resources of our own and are utterly dependent on God. It is where we are overwhelmed by God's infinite mercy.

The desert deep within our soul is a difficult place to go. It frightens us. We try to avoid it if we can. We can take care of ourselves, we think. But it is only in the desert we realize that we can't, and that we need God. And when we accept that, an oasis of riches springs forth from that desert to nourish us.

Prayer, ultimately, is about conversion, our transformation in Christ, and that occurs when we become aware of God's infinite willingness and ability to supply all that we lack. His mercy and love are greater than our sin and failure. But to know infinite goodness, we must first acknowledge what is limited and imperfect.

The desert provides this contrast, and it is where Jesus invites us in prayer. Pick up your Bible, put this book aside for a little while, and read the following Scripture passages: *Exodus 16:2-4a, 9-15; Deuteronomy 8:2a, 3; Matthew 4:1-4; Mark 6:30-44.* As you do so, notice the theme that runs through and connects these passages. What really strikes me about these biblical episodes in salvation history is not only the care God provides for the ancient Israelites in the desert, but the solidarity Jesus later shares with all his people—including us. Just like the Israelites, he was led into the desert and tempted to turn away from it. Just like all of us, he gets hungry. After relying on the word of God as his source of strength, he then leads his followers into the desert to experience the same thing.

When Jesus sees the crowd, he experiences gut-wrenching compassion for them as the Good Shepherd, and he begins to feed them, first with Wisdom—the word of God—then with bread. There is a very clear connection with the journey the pilgrim people of God have made—and are making—through the wilderness of life, relying solely on the grace of God, who sustains them with the Bread of Life.

Another point that comes across, particularly in the passage from Mark, is that of need. The apostles return to Jesus to report "all they had done and taught." Jesus doesn't say, "Good job!" Instead, he says, "Come into the desert with me." There, faced with the prospect of feeding 5,000 people, the apostles realize they can do nothing, or very little, on their own. There's a lesson in humility here—it is God who works wonders, and we can only experience them if we acknowledge that we *can't* work them. "Apart from me, you can do nothing," Jesus tells his disciples (John 15:5). We *need* God. In Jesus, this God inserted himself into human history to be one with us in Spirit as we journey through the wilderness toward the promise of eternal life.

What does this journey through the desert mean in terms of prayer? It means Jesus has been there. He knows what it's like for each and every one of us. He knows what we each need, where we each hurt. But he can only provide it if we come to him in prayer and honestly acknowledge it, and let go of our self-reliance and fear.

This is a holy hunger that only God can fully satisfy—in the wilderness. ♠

# Prayer of Invitation

Lord God, the Eternal Source of all Being, my soul hungers for you because you have sown your Word in my heart. So often, though, I lose my way because I am distracted, preoccupied, even focused on good things for the wrong reasons. My vision becomes clouded, and I feed on things that ultimately leave me empty.

Lead me by your Spirit into the desert of my soul, the secret room of my heart, where you invite me to a personal relationship with Jesus, your Son. Help me to encounter and embrace there what I truly desire, and what you truly wish to give me, in union with your Church throughout the world.

Deepen my prayer through your grace so that I may hear and heed your loving invitation, your gentle call. Help me to recognize and respond to your ever-present voice through the surrender of whatever holds me back or turns me away.

May I discover—and rediscover each day—your creating power, your saving grace, your constant presence. I wish to taste and see that you are good. Fill me with your wisdom, your food for my journey toward you.

Bring my heart into prayer, so that my whole time and being rests in you and you alone, that I may bear the fruit that your food alone provides. Lord of the harvest, feed me.

I ask all this through Christ your Son, who lives and reigns with you and the Holy Spirit, one God for ever and ever. Amen.

# The Better Part

Our love for God can be more readily stirred if we simply content ourselves to rest in the Divine Presence, in silence and peace. Often, our own tired attempts at prayer can end in frustration, and while God certainly appreciates sincere effort, prayer without a heart truly centered on God is simply recitation.

After all, do we *really* know what to pray for? Only God can see our true needs, from the perspective of eternity. As St. Paul writes, "The Spirit helps us in our weakness; for we do not know how to pray as we ought, but that very Spirit intercedes with sights too deep for words" (Romans 8:26). So, perhaps the better part is being content with listening to what God has to say to us, rather than telling God what we think we need.

Jesus imparts this message in the gospel story of Martha and Mary (Luke 10:38-42). As Jesus visited their home, Martha busied herself waiting on him and her other guests. Her sister Mary "sat at the Lord's feet and listened to what he was saying." Martha was upset by this, not because Jesus didn't appreciate what she was doing, but because she felt she was doing all the work, and she resented Mary for it. "Tell her to help me," Martha boldly demands of Jesus.

Instead, as he so often does, Jesus gently turns familiar thinking inside-out. "Martha, Martha, you are worried and distracted by many things," he says. "There is need of only one thing. Mary has chosen the better part, which will not be taken away from her."

Jesus was not criticizing Martha's effort, but leading her to pay attention to her prime motivation, which is essential for *any* effort.

She was focused on what she was *doing* rather than on the reason *why* she was doing it—to serve the Lord.

Mary, on the other hand, was completely focused on Jesus, sitting at his feet, listening to him. Her gaze was on the Lord, so she was choosing the better part. She was content with simply listening to what Jesus had to say.

In the context of Luke's entire Gospel narrative, it must be remembered that Jesus was on his way to Jerusalem, where suffering and death awaited him. Surely his heart was burdened by this, but also grieved because he knew that many in the world would continue to disregard the salvation he would soon be offering through his death and resurrection. God Incarnate was sitting among the guests at Martha's house, and so his perspective was eternal. He had come into the world to restore fallen humanity, yet it had to pain him deeply to know in advance that his gift of love would later be refused by so many, up to this very day.

From this vantage point, which seems more suitable—being fussed over by Martha, or gaining Mary's full, undivided, and loving attention and devotion? Mary, of course, had chosen the *better* part.

So it must be with us. Yes, we all have necessary work to do. But, as Christians, we must not forget *why* we do it and to what end—to build up the Kingdom of God. And yet, the building of the Kingdom does not depend solely on each one of us. God knows who we are, what we are capable of doing or not doing. In Christ, God has *already* won the victory. It is our "task" to simply enter into this truth, to be enlightened and encouraged by his Spirit of love, and to communicate that love in all we do.

First, however, we must be willing to sit like Mary at the feet of the Lord. The Spirit of love is best communicated to us when we engage in silent praise of our Creator and Redeemer—focusing solely on him, and allowing God's intimate will to enfold our hearts.

This is principally accomplished in three ways. First, there is Scripture, which invites us to listen with our hearts to God through the living Word. Scripture has a unique message for each one of us—instructing, challenging, and comforting us individually through the universal account of salvation history.

Then there is prayer, which is fueled by sincere and ardent longing for God—to seek, know, and do God's will above all else. Sure, there are distractions to contend with at times, but often the biggest distraction is the one who is praying! We must truly place ourselves in the Divine Presence, listen and unite our hearts to God's will, and refrain—for a moment, anyway—from busying about like Martha.

Finally, and most importantly, there is the Holy Eucharist, the Bread of Life, which encompasses all the rest. The Eucharist continually renews and transforms the willing heart, providing the nourishment necessary to hear and heed God's voice.

In a sense, all three of these elements are presented in Luke's account of Martha and Mary. The Eternal Word, Jesus Christ, speaks to those present. Mary listens intently, gazing on Christ, praying in the purest form of simple adoration. And all of this takes place at a meal with Christ as the guest of honor, which evokes the Eucharist that he later offers in fuller fashion the night before he died.

With this in mind, let us take every opportunity to make ourselves available to the Eternal Word, listening intently in silence and peace to what he says in the depths of our hearts while, like Mary, we pray with the gaze of adoration. Then, in Eucharistic fashion, we can go forth from the table of the Lord, having been instructed and nourished to go about the work God has entrusted to us—with Christ as our inspiration and strength.

This is the better part, sitting at the feet of Jesus, listening to him in silent praise—to guide all our ways through all our days. ♣

# The Contemplative Path

Almost everyone struggles with prayer at one time or another. During our darkest moments, God seems absolutely silent, or even absent altogether. A thousand distractions—exterior and interior—demand our attention with their taunts: "God's not here, but *we* are! Pay attention to *us*!"

We tell ourselves that nearby construction or traffic noise, a chattering acquaintance, or the Def Leppard fan next door is making it impossible for us to concentrate and contemplate. However, if we are honest with ourselves, those frustrations are usually projections of our own "inner noise" in its varied forms. They can arise from a troublesome childhood, a burdensome work situation, a strained relationship, worrisome health, or countless other issues.

Whatever the source seems to be, we feel ourselves being stirred by avarice, anger, pride, gluttony, lust, sadness, restlessness, or vainglory (Evagrius Ponticus, a fourth-century monk, said that all distracting thoughts originate from these eight). Real or imagined conversations, anxiety, guilt, fear consume us.

So, how are we supposed to pray? Where is God?

The trouble is that all those things operate on the surface of our existence. They persuade us from going any deeper—where all is silent, where all is God—to the point where we identify completely with all these thoughts and feelings. We think they define who we are. They become our "inner videos," as Martin Laird, O.S.A., calls them, and we replay them over and over in our heads until they seem to us to be the truth. But in reality, these inner videos divert our attention from the Truth that is God. So, we feel alone, isolated, alienated from God—who has, in fact, never left our side.

This entire premise is one that has come up in my own spiritual life, and it is a recurring theme with many of my spiritual directees. It is a universal phenomenon.

Thankfully, we have the wisdom of some of the very first monks and desert hermits, as well as the Early Church Fathers to guide us. Evagrius provides the key to this mystery when he says, "It is not in our power to determine whether we are disturbed by thoughts, but it is up to us to decide if they are to linger within us or not."

Laird, an Augustinian priest who teaches theology at Villanova University, has studied and written extensively on this topic. He has written two wonderful books on the subject of contemplative prayer: *Into the Silent Land: A Guide to the Christian Practice of Contemplation* (2006) and *A Sunlit Absence: Silence, Awareness, and Contemplation* (2011), both by Oxford University Press. In the latter, he writes that though God is the very ground and breath of our being, we are largely ignorant of this because of "the constant inner noise and chatter that creates and sustains the illusion of being separate from God. . . . Our culture for the most part trains us to keep our attention riveted to this surface noise, which in turn maintains the illusion of God as a distant object for which we must seek as for something we are convinced we lack. One of the great mysteries of the contemplative path is the discovery that, when the veils of separation drop, we see that the God we have been seeking has already found us, knows us, and sustains us in being from all eternity."

In contemplation, Laird says, we learn to submerge ourselves beneath the surface chatter of our lives—thoughts and feelings that come and go—to experience in our innermost depths the God through whom "we live and move and have our being" (Acts 17:28). If we simply allow ourselves to sink into the Divine Presence that permeates our lives, we stop being reactive to all those surface thoughts and feelings that can distress us and lead to so much trouble and conflict in our world. We have, he says, "highly habituated emotional styles and lifestyles that keep us constantly reacting to life like victimizing victims, ever more convinced that the videos that shape our awareness are in fact true." However, "the life of stillness gradually heals this split and leads us into wide open fields where buried treasure lies" (cf. Matthew 13:45-46).

Laird really says nothing new (and neither have I). However, he does a remarkable job of pulling together and placing the ancient wisdom of the early monks and Church Fathers into a contemporary context. He helps us understand that our difficulties in prayer are not obstacles to overcome but opportunities to surrender to what is, thereby piercing the surface of our self-identifying thoughts and emotions, and entering into the awareness of the presence of God who is all in all (cf. 1 Corinthians 15:28; Ephesians 1:23).

It is really about interior surrender, a Gospel precept presented in a fresh manner. As the Psalmist writes: "I have calmed and quieted my soul, like a weaned child with its mother; my soul is like the weaned child that is with me" (Psalm 131). 🌰

# Mary, Our Partner in Prayer

*[After the ascension of Jesus, his disciples returned to Jerusalem.] When they had entered the city, they went to the room upstairs where they were staying, Peter, and John, and James, and Andrew, Philip and Thomas, Bartholomew and Matthew, James son of Alphaeus, and Simon the Zealot, and Judas son of James. All these were constantly devoting themselves to prayer, together with certain women, including Mary the mother of Jesus, as well as his brothers. When the day of Pentecost had come, they were all together in one place. And suddenly from heaven there came a sound like the rush of a violent wind, and it filled the entire house where they were sitting. Divided tongues, as of fire, appeared among them, and a tongue rested on each of them. All of them were filled with the Holy Spirit and began to speak in other languages, as the Spirit gave them ability.*

—Acts of the Apostles 1:13-14; 2:1-4

Most of us, at one time or another, have likely implored someone, "Pray for me," or have promised someone, "I will pray for you." These are expressions of faith in a God who cares for us, but they also communicate the hope we have in one another as believers. We draw strength from knowing that we are united with one another in prayer. So we keep prayer lists. We form prayer chains. We join prayer groups. We participate in pilgrimages. And, of course, we come together in the Liturgy—especially the Eucharist—to pray for the world as the Body of Christ and offer ourselves as a spiritual sacrifice. We believe Jesus' words in Matthew's Gospel: "Where two or three are gathered in my name, I am there among them" (18:20).

Whether we pray together or alone, of course, we do so not only as the faithful on earth in communion with one another, but also with the saints in heaven and the souls in purgatory. We are never alone. We are all *partners in prayer*, imploring the gifts of the Holy Spirit, drawing strength from Christ, and seeking guidance during our earthly journey toward God the Father.

When we pray the rosary, for example—either individually or as a group—we certainly honor Mary, who is the Mother of Jesus and the Mother of the Church, the Body of Christ. When we pray the *Hail Mary*, we acclaim the Mother of God, using the words spoken by the angel Gabriel at the Annunciation and those addressed to her by her cousin Elizabeth at the time of the Visitation. We also ask her to pray for us, saying, "Pray for us sinners now and at the hour of our death." Mary is certainly our foremost partner in prayer.

However, we do not simply pray *to* her, asking her to intercede for us. We also pray *with* her as the first Christian disciples did, as recounted above in the passage from the Acts of the Apostles. Mary prays with us, directing our gaze toward Christ, and preparing us for the continual outpouring of the Holy Spirit upon all the members of the Body of Christ. After the risen Jesus had ascended to the Father, all the apostles, along with some women, Mary, and other relatives of Jesus, went back to Jerusalem to the Upper Room—the same room where Jesus instituted the Eucharist during the Last Supper the night before he died on the Cross. There, we are told, they "were constantly devoting themselves to prayer." Mary prayed with all of them as they awaited Jesus' promise to send the Holy Spirit upon them.

Later, during the feast of Pentecost, we are told that "they were together in one place," and "all of them were filled with the Holy Spirit," which enabled them to proclaim the Good News.

Tradition asserts that Mary was present for all this. Just as the Holy Spirit had descended upon her at the Annunciation to give birth to Christ, now the Holy Spirit descends upon the first Christian assembly in Mary's presence to give birth to the Church, children of the Father as one Body of Christ.

Mary had *already* been overshadowed by the Holy Spirit at the Incarnation. She had been with Jesus from the moment of his conception to his last breath. The rest of the disciples, however, had not yet received the Holy Spirit. They were still waiting, and were not sure what to expect. Imagine their confusion and anxiety considering all that had happened in the preceding days—the crucifixion of their Teacher, his Resurrection, his post-Resurrection appearances to them, his mandate to "go and make disciples of all nations" (Matthew 28:19), and his Ascension. They were not sure what it all meant, or how they should respond. They were afraid, the Gospel of John tells us.

Already a recipient of the Holy Spirit and the perfect model of faithfulness to God's Word, Mary remained with the apostles and other disciples to strengthen and prepare them for what lay ahead. As Pope John Paul II said during a general audience in 1997, "Unlike those in the Upper Room who were waiting in fearful expectation, Mary, fully aware of the importance of her Son's promise to the disciples, helped the community to be well-disposed to the coming of the Paraclete." She was involved "in preparing the minds and hearts of those around her."

She was their *partner in prayer*, and *remains* so for us.

The passage from the Acts of the Apostles is the last mention of Mary in the New Testament. She was the only follower of Christ who was with him at every stage of his life—from conception and birth to his death, and now his new birth in the first community of believers who will carry on his work in the world as the Church. As John Paul II said, "Mary's prayer has particular significance in the Christian community: It fosters the coming of the Spirit, imploring his action in the hearts of the disciples and in the world. Just as in the Incarnation, the Spirit had formed the *physical* body of Christ in her virginal womb, now in the Upper Room the same Spirit comes down to give life to the Mystical Body" (May 28, 1997, general audience). . . . "As Mother of the Church, Mary continually brings to birth children for the Mystical Body of her Son. She does so through her intercession, imploring upon them the inexhaustible outpouring of the Spirit" (Encyclical *Rosarium Virginis Mariae*).

Mary is our partner in prayer—from the moment of our birth in Christ at Baptism until the hour of our death. She prays not only *for* us, but *with* us, just as she did with the first community of believers in the Upper Room at Pentecost.

To illustrate this point further, let us take a brief look at one episode from each of the four sets of mysteries of the rosary. We've already examined Pentecost, the third Glorious Mystery. If we turn to the Visitation, the second Joyful Mystery, we encounter Elizabeth crying out with joy as the child John leaps in her womb at Mary's greeting (Luke 1:39-55). Mary, who had come to assist Elizabeth in her old age in giving birth to John the Baptist, responds to her cousin with the words of the *Magnificat*, the ancient hymn from the Gospel of Luke which the Church sings at Vespers. As John Paul II wrote, the *Magnificat* is an "inspired profession of faith, in which Mary's response to the revealed word is expressed with the religious and poetical exultation of her whole being toward God. The Church, which even amid trials and tribulations does not cease repeating with Mary the words of the *Magnificat*, is sustained by the power of God's truth" (Encyclical *Redemptoris Mater*). As we can see, Mary was not only *physically* present to Elizabeth. She was also *spiritually* present, praying with her—and that prayer continues through the ages in the voices of people everywhere who pray the *Magnificat*.

In the Wedding Feast at Cana, the second Luminous Mystery of the rosary, "Mary places herself between her son and mankind in the reality of their wants, needs, and sufferings" when she tells Jesus that "they have no wine" (John 2:1-5). Also, when she says to the servants, saying, "Do whatever he tells you," Mary "presents herself as the spokeswoman of her son's will" (*Redemptoris Mater*). Here again, Mary prays *with* the people, presenting their needs to Jesus, and conveying to them how important it is to listen to him.

Finally, at the Crucifixion, the fifth Sorrowful Mystery, Mary and the beloved disciple stand with Jesus who has been nailed to the cross. Jesus says to Mary, "Here is your son," and to the beloved disciple, "Here is your mother" (John 19:26-27). Here, he entrusts all disciples to Mary, and calls all disciples to honor Mary as Mother of the Church. In essence, he makes them prayer partners.

Aspects of intercession or partnership are evident in all four of these mysteries—the Visitation, the Wedding Feast at Cana, the Crucifixion, and Pentecost. If we look more closely at each one of them, we can see that Mary makes herself prayer partners with four distinct groups of people. In the Visitation, it is *relatives*. At the Wedding Feast at Cana, it is *friends*. At the Crucifixion, it is *family*—both physically and spiritually. And at Pentecost, it is the entire *community* of believers. Mary joins herself in prayer to *all* these people—both at that time and today. She prays with and for relatives, friends, families, and the entire Church.

We participate as partners in prayer through the reading of Scripture and through such practices as praying the rosary—which Mary, in essence, "recited" by the very experiences of her life. We pray with Mary in the secret recesses of our hearts, pondering as she did the unfolding of these mysteries in our own lives. And we pray with Mary in the liturgy, such as by singing the *Magnificat* during Evening Prayer of the Divine Office, and especially at the Eucharist. We must recall that through the Incarnation, when the Holy Spirit first descended upon Mary, Jesus, the Word made Flesh, received his earthly flesh and blood from her. It is this same humanity he gives to us sacramentally during the celebration of the Eucharist.

All of this points to the timeless nature of Mary's prayer. Pentecost was not a one-time event in the history of salvation. "Pentecost is still happening," said John Paul II, in a homily in 1980. "Every place where the disciples of the Lord gather is an extension of that original [Pentecost]." As the Second Vatican Council's *Lumen Gentium* stated, "The entire body of the faithful pours forth instant supplications to the Mother of God and Mother of men that she, who aided the beginnings of the Church by her prayers, may now ... intercede before her Son in the fellowship of all the saints, until all families of people, whether they are honored with the title of Christian or whether they still do not know the Savior, may be happily gathered together in peace and harmony into one people of God" (*LG* 69).

So, Mary remains with us as our partner in prayer—today and each day of our earthly sojourn. "In our time, she is no less present to the Church than she was at Pentecost, gathered with the apostles in prayer. With her prayer and presence, she will surely support the new evangelization just as she supported the first. In times of difficulty and pain, Mary has been an unfailing refuge for those seeking peace and healing. In churches, chapels and homes, the image of Mary reminds people of her loving presence and her maternal protection" (John Paul II, *Ecclesia in Oceania*).

Like the first Christians, let us devote ourselves to prayer together with Mary, the mother of Jesus. Let us make Mary our prayer partner, praying not only *to* her but *with* her as we contemplate the mysteries of Christ. Let us place *ourselves* in the Upper Room at Pentecost, imploring the gifts of the Holy Spirit, so that "the prayer of the Church is sustained by the prayer of Mary and united with it in hope" (*Catechism of the Catholic Church*, 2679).

Let us say together: *"Mary, pray for us,"* and believe with our hearts that *she* is saying to us: *"I'll pray for you."* ❧

# Ordinary Prayer and Faith

A sk and you will receive, Jesus tells his disciples. However, he also says that we are to ask in accordance with his will: "If you ask anything of the Father in my name, he will give it to you. Until now you have not asked for anything in my name. Ask and you will receive, so that your joy may be complete" (John 16:23-24).

The liturgical seasons of Advent, Christmas, Lent, and Easter provide us with much to anticipate and celebrate in terms of our Christian faith. But how do we live that out the rest of the year? Ordinary Time, after all, comprises well over half of the year. Feasts and solemnities aside, for the most part we are called to find Christ in the day-to-day, unremarkable, ordinariness of human living.

A passage from Mark's Gospel (9:14-29) offers some guidance in this regard, pointing us toward the importance of prayer and faith in our *daily* lives. Although it may be argued, on one level, that what Jesus does in this particular passage—healing a boy by expelling the demon tormenting him—is anything but ordinary, the overall message is one of entrusting *everything* to God through prayer and faith. After all, demons such as doubt, despair, spiritual idleness, and so many others are *daily* companions, tempting us to lose all hope in a God who seems absent or oblivious, as we aimlessly flail away, seemingly at the mercy of life's frustrations and disappointments.

Such is the scene at the outset of this Gospel passage. Things are out of control. A man has brought his possessed son to Jesus' disciples to be healed. However, regardless of what they try, nothing works. A fierce argument breaks out. This is the setting into which Jesus appears. After finding out what all the commotion is about, Jesus expresses exasperation with all of them. "You faithless generation, how much longer must I be among you? How much longer must I put up with you?"

But Jesus does not throw up his hands and simply walk away. "Bring [the boy] to me," he says. When this is done, the spirit possessing him flings the boy into convulsions. His father says to Jesus, "If you are able to do anything, have pity on us and help us."

Once again, Jesus is taken aback. "*If you are able!*" he retorts. "All things can be done for the one who believes." This is the key moment upon which the whole event turns. The father acknowledges his lack of faith while at the same time expressing an earnest desire for more faith. In other words, he prays.

"I believe; help my unbelief!" he says.

Jesus then expels the unclean spirit. Order is restored from chaos.

Later, when Jesus is alone with his disciples, they ask him why they were not able to do what he did. "This kind can come out only through prayer," he responds.

Prayer expresses our faith. Other things (such as works of mercy) do as well, but prayer is foremost because it acknowledges our need to be in right relationship with God—it *is* our relationship with God. Prayer is God's invitation to dedicate our time and being to a fuller appreciation of the divine, so that our vision broadens and our hearts expand with love. It is a lifelong rhythm of listening and responding to God's call for conversion of heart—personally and communally.

Prayer is not a means by which we attempt to persuade God to *give us* this or that, or to *do* this or that. It is open, honest, full-hearted conversation with a God who loves us beyond measure, so that we may become our true selves in the divine image. We pray *to be changed into who God wishes us to be*—not orphans, but children of God.

Jesus instructs us to pray always, so as not to lose heart (Luke 18:1). Many times throughout the gospels, after expelling a demon or healing someone, his parting words are: "Your faith has saved you." Wealth, honor, health, success, and so many other things are all well and good, as far as they go. And as dutiful Christians, we may strive for perfection to the point of exhaustion. But in the end, it is solely *faith* that saves us—faith in the unfathomable and ineffable mystery of God's indisputable and merciful presence in our lives despite what the world's values and circumstances seem to suggest. After all, as the Letter to the Hebrews famously states: "Faith is the assurance of things hoped for, the conviction of things not seen" (11:1).

So, we must pray as did the apostles, "Lord, increase our faith!" (Luke 17:5), or as did the possessed boy's father: "I believe; help my unbelief!" These are honest expressions of acknowledged incompleteness. In them, we state our desire to be freed from whatever holds us back from God. Even when we are in the grips of the deepest doubt, we can confidently pray for more faith.

"Ask and you will receive," Jesus says in John's Gospel. True faith is a gift that cannot be refused to the one who prays for it. In this way, we find Christ in the day-to-day, unremarkable, ordinariness of human living. "Remember," Jesus says, "I am with you always, to the end of the age" (Matthew 28:20).

So, let us pray—this day and every day, all day and for all days. Everything is possible to one who has faith—even grasping what seems just beyond our reach. Faith is what completes our joy, and as Christians, that is anything but ordinary. ♠

# The Body of Christ

# Appearances

*We look not at what can be seen but at what cannot be seen;*
*for what can be seen is temporary, but what cannot be seen is eternal.*
—2 Corinthians 4:18

Appearances can indeed deceive. Reality is often disguised, requiring a depth of perception beyond ordinary means. The sun rises in the east and sets in the west each day, seeming to cross from one end of the sky to the other. We know that's not really true, despite all appearances. The sun is stationary. The revolution of the Earth, which in turn orbits the sun, makes it *seem* as though the sun is moving. In reality, the Earth is moving.

Scientific knowledge helps us understand the universe which we see and live in. The knowledge of faith helps us enter into the mystery of the spiritual reality that underlies and infuses the universe which we see and live in.

For Catholics, of course, there is no greater mystery than that of the Eucharist, which is the source and summit of our faith. In the Eucharist, we receive the Body, Blood, Soul, and Divinity of Jesus Christ under the species of ordinary bread and wine. What we see is *not* all we get! And we get more than we could ever imagine.

Eucharistic themes are replete throughout Scripture, and they unfold for us during the liturgical year at Mass in the Liturgy of the Word. In 1 Kings 19:4-8, for example, the prophet Elijah is sustained and strengthened for his journey by food and drink provided by God. In John 6:41-51, Jesus tells a skeptical crowd: "I am the living bread that came down from heaven. Whoever eats of this bread will live forever; and the bread that I will give for the life of the world is my flesh."

Meanwhile, Ephesians 4:30-5:2 conveys to us the true meaning of Communion with God the Father, Son, and Holy Spirit: "Put away from you all bitterness and wrath and anger and wrangling and slander, together with all malice, and be kind to one another, tenderhearted, forgiving one another, as God in Christ has forgiven you. Therefore be imitators of God, as beloved children, and live in love, as Christ loved us and gave himself up for us." In other words, we receive Christ to *become* Christ. If we are what we eat, as the saying goes, we must become what, in faith, we receive in the Eucharist, as St. Augustine said: "You are the mystery that is placed on the Lord's table. You receive the mystery that is yourself. To that which you are, you will respond."

Those who confronted Jesus in the sixth chapter of John's Gospel, murmuring about his claims of being "the bread that came down from heaven," had not yet opened their hearts to receive the knowledge of faith and see the spiritual reality of what he was saying. Their focus was only on what they could *see* with their own eyes. "Is this not Jesus, the son of Joseph, whose father and mother we know? How can he now say, 'I have come down from heaven'?" They saw only the species in front of them, not the Presence. Appearance deceived them.

People of that time, incidentally, also believed the sun revolved around the Earth. Humanity had a lot to learn on many different levels. We still do:

*Now we see in a mirror, dimly,*
*but then we will see face to face.*
*Now I know only in part;*
*then I will know fully,*
*even as I have been fully known.*
　　　　　—1 Corinthians 13:12

# This Is My Body

*Why do the nations conspire,*
*and the peoples plot in vain?*
—Psalm 2:1

Why do you suppose, when we speak of the Church, so often we end up speaking of it merely in human terms?

We all do it. It is human nature, we might say. It is our nature to view the Church as we do other "institutions." It is something to influence, or be influenced by. It is something to exert authority, or something by which authority can be acquired.

How often do we attempt to define the great unknown only by what we are capable of perceiving? Too often, it seems, we view the spiritual through the lens of the political. We see division rather than union.

Right versus wrong.

Us versus them.

Man versus woman.

Rich versus poor.

Black versus white.

Democrat versus Republican.

Conservative versus liberal.

Traditional versus progressive.

Catholic versus Protestant.

The list goes on.

If this is what the Church is—to borrow a phrase from Flannery O'Connor—then to hell with it.

But this is *not* what the Church is. We know that what Isaiah the prophet tells us is true: "My thoughts are not your thoughts, nor are your ways my ways, says the Lord" (Isaiah 55:8).

However, like Martha in the Gospel of Luke (10:38-42), we become distracted, perturbed, and adamant. "You are worried and distracted by many things," Jesus tells us. "There is need of only one thing."

This one thing necessary captured the undivided attention of Martha's sister Mary, who sat at the feet of Christ. The Church, after all, is not a mere human institution or political organization. It is none other than a Person—Christ himself, who invites us to share in his divinity through the Eucharist. With him, in him, and through him, we comprise the Body of Christ. *This* is the Church.

"He assumed our nature in order that by becoming man he might make us divine," St. Thomas Aquinas tells us. "When he took our flesh he dedicated the whole of its substance to our salvation."

"Take it," Jesus says to his disciples after blessing, breaking, and giving them bread at the Last Supper, the night before he delivered his life for the world. "This is my body" (cf. Matthew 26:6, Mark 14:22; Luke 22:19; 1 Corinthians 11:24).

The Eucharist, then, is our binding force with God and one another. It is our truest identity. Fed with Christ, what is human becomes transformed into his Body, which the Church not only celebrates but gives to the world. It is the Church's mission to transform the world by transforming you and me into Christ, who both transforms and transcends all human institutions—often in ways in which we are unable to see, except through the eyes of faith.

"The Real Presence of Christ," Pope Emeritus Benedict XVI says, "makes each one of us his 'house' and all together we form his

Church, the spiritual building of which St. Peter speaks, 'Come to him, to that living stone, rejected by men but in God's sight chosen and precious, and like living stones be yourselves built into a spiritual house'" (1 Peter 2:4-5).

As baptized Christians, corporately and individually, we are made one with the Body of Christ, who mystically works through us all as the Church—human warts and all.

As St. Paul says, "There is no longer Jew or Greek, there is no longer slave or free, there is no longer male and female; for all of you are one in Christ Jesus. The bread that we break, is it not a sharing in the body of Christ? Because there is one bread, we who are many are one body, for we all partake of the one bread" (Galatians 3:38, 1 Corinthians 10:16-17).

Like Mary, who sat and listened at the feet of Jesus, we must fix our attention on Christ, who is that one thing necessary who unites all. Then the kingdom of God is among us as the Church. Viewed through this lens, we see union rather than division, and the Church defines *us* rather than vice-versa.

In this way we see Christ as he is—the divine instrument of human salvation in which we all share.

Then, like shoots of the olive, we gather around his table as God's children.

"Take it. This is my body." ♣

# Food for Thought

T he Church and the Eucharist are inseparable. Holding the key to this mystery is 1 Corinthians 11:23-26, the oldest written account we're aware of that describes the institution of the Lord's Supper. The passage explains the practice of the Early Church as received from Christ and handed on to us through the apostles.

The Paschal Mystery—the passion, death, and resurrection of Christ—is the central and sustaining event in the faith of the People of God and life of the Church. The gift and mystery of the bread and cup was entrusted by Christ to the Church—through the apostles—at the Last Supper which we commemorate on Holy Thursday of the Paschal Triduum. There, and now, Jesus says, "Do this in remembrance of me." As Pope John Paul II points out in *Ecclesia de Eucharistia*, the Last Supper foreshadows what follows over the next three days.

The Eucharist, then, signifies and makes fully present this singular event, uniting it with all eternity. This ultimate sacrament of the unity of the People of God expresses what it is and what is achieved by it—the salvation of mankind through Christ's gift of self on the cross. As we sing during the celebration of the Eucharist, "When we eat this bread and drink this cup, we proclaim your death, O Lord, until you come again."

If, as St. Augustine said, we become what we receive in the Eucharist, then we offer ourselves with, in, and through Christ as his Body for the salvation of the world. As the Church, we pray *as Christ* through the Holy Spirit that all may become one body, and one spirit in him as a total offering to God the Father.

So, it is through the Eucharist that the Church becomes a sign and sacrament of humanity's salvation as obtained by Christ through the paschal mystery we celebrate at every Mass. As the Body of Christ, we are a *living sacrifice of praise* through Whom we receive and through Whom we are. ♣

# Saints, All

**Y**ou are not alone. No matter how you may feel at the moment or what you are facing at this point in your life, this is God's primary message to humanity each day of the year—throughout all of history. In a more intense way, we celebrate this reality liturgically on the Solemnity of All the Saints on November 1 each year.

In the church at Saint Meinrad Archabbey, where I live in southern Indiana, monks and guests are surrounded by reminders of this as we gather each day around the Altar of the Lord. The lives of the saints are depicted in the stained glass windows and shrines of the church, and the relics of a good number of saints are present in the sanctuary.

However, when speaking of the saints, we refer not only to those officially recognized as such by the Church. We mean *all* the faithful, past and present, from the entire world—as St. John writes in the Book of Revelation, "a great multitude that no one could count, from every nation, from all tribes and peoples and languages" (Revelation 7:9).

In the celebration of the Eucharist, time and space are transcended, and the Mystical Body of Christ stands united—including all who have gone before us and all who are still on their earthly journey. This communion is *always* a reality, but is *especially* present to us in the celebration of the Eucharist—anytime and anywhere it is celebrated.

In the Eucharist, we gather as children of God to gain a foretaste of what is to come—as illuminated in John's vision and promised to us by Christ in the Beatitudes. Indeed, we are called not only to *join* the saints in their praise of God, but to *become* saints through our praise of God. As Pope Emeritus Benedict XVI says, "To become saints means to fulfill completely what we already are, raised to the dignity of God's adopted children in Christ Jesus."

This is the hope that makes us pure—and *together* we share it. 🌿

# Nations Shall Come to Your Light

Too often, it seems, Christianity is drawn into the political arena, where it becomes a sparring partner in the daily round of partisan debates. There, it takes a beating, but also is just as capable of delivering stinging blows (sometimes self-inflicted).

The Mass readings in January each year for the celebration of the Solemnity of the Epiphany of the Lord (Isaiah 60:1-6; Ephesians 3:2-3a, 5-6; Matthew 2:1-12) invite us to step back for a moment and reassess who we truly are, what the Church is truly about, and which battles are worth fighting. Three themes come to mind:

1. The Church is **UNIVERSAL**. God's offer of salvation through Jesus Christ belongs to *all* people of every race, nation, and age. It is not an exclusive club bestowing privilege on the few; rather, it is the Body of Christ whose *responsibility* it is to draw all humankind into God's embrace. All three Scripture passages cited above point to this truth. Isaiah tells us that "nations shall come to your light," while Paul emphasizes that the Gentiles (the "outsiders" in the early days of Christianity) are "fellow heirs, members of the same body, and sharers in the promise in Christ Jesus through the gospel." Finally, the magi in Matthew's Gospel are foreigners, the first "Gentiles" to see and come to the light of Christ.

2. We are a **PILGRIM** Church, journeying like the magi in this world in search of a personal encounter with our Savior, to whom we offer our gifts of public praise. The magi experienced the newborn Savior, but they had yet to experience the crucified and risen Christ. We, too, *journey in stages* toward the promise of Christ, and we do so as a *community* of believers. As Isaiah prophesies, "All gather together, they come to you; your sons shall come from far away, and your daughters shall be carried

46

on their nurses' arms."

3. We are meant to be a **SIGN** to the world of God's offer of salvation through a personal encounter with Christ. Epiphany means "manifestation," and our mission as the Church is to make visible the redeeming work of Christ as expressed by the Gospel. We are stewards of God's grace. We are that shining star by whose light others should be drawn into the wonderful mystery of Christ. Sometimes, yes, shining brightly means a willingness to step into the ring and fight for what is true. But let us not forget what makes Christians unique, and that is daily living governed by:

> The Ten Commandments
>
> The Eight Beatitudes
>
> The Three Theological Virtues
>
> The Four Cardinal Virtues
>
> The Seven Gifts of the Holy Spirit
>
> The 12 Fruits of the Holy Spirit
>
> The Seven Corporal Works of Mercy
>
> The Seven Spiritual Works of Mercy
>
> And, of course, prayer, fasting, and almsgiving

Scripture, tradition, and the sacramental life of the Church as the worshipping Body of Christ are meant to infuse us with that light that must be *seen* by others. More than going through the motions and fulfilling obligations is required. We must truly come to the Light and receive it in our hearts in order to make it seen. If it cannot be seen, what is the point? And I would propose that the ray of light most capable of penetrating deeply into the heart of another is Christian **JOY**, one of the fruits of the Holy Spirit. As the Gospel tells us, the magi were "overwhelmed with joy" at seeing the star.

Let us pray together, and for one another, at the dawn of each new year and each new day, so that our joy may shine brightly throughout the world, drawing all humankind into God's embrace as we journey toward the Savior and manifest his grace as the Body of Christ. In the words of Isaiah, "Lift your eyes and look around. Then you shall see and be radiant; your heart shall thrill and rejoice." ♣

# Nothing Will Be Wasted

*When they were satisfied, Jesus told his disciples,*
*"Gather up the fragments left over, so that nothing may be lost."*

—John 6:12

We waste an awful lot. Food, time, energy, water, money. The list goes on. Ours is a disposable society. Everything is important, but nothing matters much.

We waste words. Many speak. Few say anything. No wonder so few listen.

We waste opportunities. They fly by every second of our lives. Every once in a while, we grab one and make the most of it. Most pass by unnoticed, never to return.

We waste knowledge, emotions, actions.

We waste joy, sadness, courage, fear, conviction, uncertainty, pleasure, pain.

We waste people. If we're honest, we'll admit we often pay attention only to those whom we like, and who like us.

We waste death. Life is cheap.

We waste the grandeur of mystery, the glorious gifts that drench us from above each and every moment we spend on this earth. The Kingdom of Heaven is budding all around us, but we see dimly.

More than anything, we waste love. God's love. Love of ourselves. The love of others.

*But all is not lost. Not even close.*

At the beginning of the sixth chapter of John's Gospel Jesus feeds 5,000 people. All they had were five barley loaves (the food of the poor) and two fish. It wasn't much. In fact, it wasn't anything at all. They needed food, but had too little. Jesus fed them all. They had their fill and were satisfied.

Often overlooked, though, is this passage: "When they were satisfied, Jesus told his disciples, 'Gather up the fragments left over, so that nothing may be lost.'" Some translations present the last phrase as: "so that nothing will be *wasted*." Either way, it's an important sentence. Why do you think Jesus cared about all the leftovers? Why did the writer of the Gospel feel it necessary to report this? As the end of John says, Jesus did many other things that were never recorded. This one was.

Much more than a meal is going on here. Jesus is providing more than food for the hungry. These acts—this mystery—signifies something else, something much greater.

God provides for those who need, for those who have nothing (which is really each one of us, in one respect or another). God gives us Himself. Jesus gathers us, feeds us, and fills us with bread from heaven. The Body of Christ then becomes what it receives. We are what we eat, as the saying goes.

Then, when we are filled, Jesus instructs *us* as his Body: "Gather up the fragments left over, so that nothing will be wasted"—fragments, scraps, crumbs, crusts, tidbits, particles.

Garbage, waste, trash is what we usually call them.

But nothing will be lost, nothing wasted, Jesus says. *Nothing.*

At Mass, after all have received Communion, the priest, deacon, and/or Extraordinary Ministers of Holy Communion consume whatever remains—they don't throw it out. Nothing is wasted.

"I am the living bread that came down from heaven. . . . Whoever eats me will live because of me," Jesus says (John 6:51, 57). We are fed by the very life of Jesus, and our lives as Christ are commissioned to feed the lives of others, to gather all the fragments, so that none will be lost.

Nothing will be wasted. No matter our need, nor how little we seem to have.

Not food, time, energy, water, nor money.

Not words.

Not opportunities.

Not knowledge, emotions, nor actions.

Not joy, sadness, courage, fear, conviction, uncertainty, pleasure, nor pain.

Not people. Those we like, nor don't like. Those who like us, and those who don't.

Not even death will be wasted. The Resurrected Christ in us gathers all the barley loaves of the poor, all the fragments and crumbs, whatever seems small and useless, and makes us One.

Nothing that we have, do, or are is wasted. Everything belongs. *It all matters*—this grandeur of mystery, this glorious gift that drenches us from above each and every moment. We may still see dimly, but the Kingdom of Heaven buds all around us—especially in all the leftovers.

God's love is not wasted. Not one crumb, no matter how crusty. Taste and see. ♠

# Touching the Wounds that Heal

Jesus appears in the midst of the disciples gathered together on the first day of the week—a Sunday—to bring them peace and the promise of reconciliation in the Holy Spirit (cf. John 20:19-31). When the apostle Thomas, who was not present at the time, finds the testimony of his companions—"We have seen the Lord"—difficult to believe, he does not mock their account in a spirit of cynicism. Rather, he honestly questions in a spirit of openness and faith. After all, he *does* come back the following Sunday.

Once again, Jesus appears in their midst, offering peace, and then inviting Thomas personally to touch the sanctifying wounds that crucified him and redeemed the world. Thomas responds by proclaiming, "My Lord and my God!"

Such passages (along with Acts 2:42-47 and 1 Peter 1:3-9, among others) offer us a profound vision of the Early Church that has been passed down to us. Together, we gather on the first day of the week, devoted to the teaching of the apostles, fellowship with one another, the Eucharist, and communal worship and prayer around the Word made Flesh.

We come with all our wounds and our doubts, but we come nonetheless to proclaim, "My Lord and my God!" Jesus is in our very midst, offering peace and reconciliation in the Holy Spirit, and inviting us to touch the wounds that heal us.

The message is this: We don't have to be whole and know all the answers to believe. We only need to gather in a spirit of openness and faith, willing to embrace our own and one another's woundedness within the Body of Christ.

In this way, God, in his great mercy, gives us new birth to a living hope through the resurrection of Jesus Christ.

*Blessed are those who have not seen and yet have come to believe!* ⚜

# Connectivity

S cripture offers us numerous reminders of how the Holy Spirit works in the Body of Christ. The message is this: *We are never alone.* "I will not leave you orphaned," Jesus promises (John 14:15-21). In baptism, we are sanctified—claimed—as God's children and sealed with the Holy Spirit. Through the sacrament of confirmation (cf. Acts 8:5-8, 14-17), we are fortified by the Holy Spirit to live more fully in faith, hope, and love.

The Spirit is not a concept, but a *Person*—the third Person of the One and Triune God who animates and enlightens God's Temple, the Church as the Body of Christ, and our individual souls. Jesus calls the Spirit the "Advocate" who will be with us always. The Greek term for this word supplies us with a traditional definition—a supporter or defender, like a defense attorney. It also means an intercessor, a mediator, spokesperson, and a comforter or consoler.

However, there is a deeper meaning—that of a teacher or witness. The Spirit of Truth instructs and provides evidence through *personal presence.* This means that Jesus is more fully present to us than he ever was to his disciples in his own time and place. Then, he was only present to *them.* Now, he is present to *all*, throughout time and eternity.

In Christ and through the Holy Spirit, we are made friends of God. We are all connected—the ultimate social network.

Because of this, we have the Advocate—in prayer, in the Eucharist, in the other sacraments, in Scripture, in the ministers of the Church, and its living Tradition, in one another, and in our hearts. The Spirit—coequal and coeternal with Father and Son—is the reason for our hope.

Brought to life in the Spirit through the death and resurrection of Christ (cf. 1 Peter 3:15-18), we have faith in yesterday, hope in tomorrow, and love for today. We become one with the Holy Trinity, now and forever. Amen. ⚜

# The Breath of God

T he Holy Spirit is the very breath of God who enlivens and enlightens all creation. The Third Person of the Holy Trinity, sent by the Risen Son through the Father, breathes life into the Church so that the world may live, move, and have its entire being in God (cf. Acts 17:28).

Filled with the joy of the Resurrection, this is the message and mission of Pentecost for the Church—2,000 years ago, and today.

Wind and Spirit are associated with one another throughout Scripture. This analogy—and reality—is meant to remind us that we live by the very breath—or Spirit—of God. The Spirit—wind—is stirred up whenever God is creating or achieving one of his "mighty acts."

The first verses of Genesis tell us that a "wind from God" swept over the chaotic and dark nothingness to bring order and light and life to the universe. In Genesis 2:7, God forms man and blows into him the "breath of life." In Genesis 8:1, God makes a "wind blow over the earth" to chase away the deadly waters of the Great Flood. In Exodus 14:21, acting through Moses, God's wind sweeps over the Red Sea to part the waters and grant the Israelites safe passage. In Ezekiel 37, the prophet in a vision imparts God's breath to restore life in a valley of dry bones.

At Pentecost (cf. Acts 2:1-11; 1 Corinthians 12:3b-7, 12-13; John 20:19-23), these signs take on new meaning in God's mighty act of breathing life—the Holy Spirit—into the Church through Christ. A mighty wind, tongues of fire, and the very breath of Jesus fill his disciples with the divine life necessary to go out and fill the world with his presence.

As he sent them with the Spirit, so he sends us. The gift of the Holy Spirit continues the work of God through our service of one another. So, as the Church, the Body of Christ, let us breathe God's peace into the world and enflame it with the fire of his love—for many though we are, we all drink of the one Spirit! ❧

# Do This in Memory of Me

"**R**emember," Moses tells the Israelites (Deuteronomy 8:2-3, 14b-16a). *Remember* how God has directed you, guided you through every affliction, strengthened you, protected and delivered you, and how he has sustained your life with food and drink from heaven. "Do not forget," Moses instructs the people, whose long and trying journey to the Promised Land prefigures our Christian journey in this world.

*Remember* in this sense means quite simply: "Trust God." *Trust* that you are in his presence every step of the way, and that he will care and provide for you. *Trust* that you are being fed spiritually through Word and Sacrament with food and drink from heaven. *Trust* that we, though many, participate in the very life of Christ, the Bread of Life who gave his life that we might live forever (cf. 1 Corinthians 10:16-17; John 6:51-58).

This is how we are to recall the reality of God's presence in our lives, and share Christ's very real presence in a unique and special way during the Eucharist, where time and eternity meet. It is important to keep in mind that the passage from St. John's Gospel cited above follows shortly after the multiplication of the loaves. After miraculously feeding the crowds with only five loaves and two fish, the people hungrily pursue Jesus. And he tells them, "I am the living bread that came down from heaven. Whoever eats of this bread will live forever."

*Remember.* ♠

# Conversion

# Turn, Turn, Turn

"Repent, for the Kingdom of Heaven has come near," declares John the Baptist (Matthew 3:1-12). He then goes on to say, "Bear fruit worthy of repentance."

This is really the heart of God's everlasting message to us: Turn to the Word made flesh, the person of Jesus Christ. Too often, it seems, we limit Christianity by associating it too closely with our own social and political agendas. It becomes what we *do* rather than who we *are*.

First, though, we are called to repent—or *turn*—to the "Kingdom of Heaven" (the term used by the ancient Israelites to avoid mentioning the unutterable name of God). This means committing oneself to conversion of heart. *Then*, John the Baptist says, we must bear fruit as outward *evidence* of our inward turning, or conversion. This is discipleship, and it renders us capable of genuinely welcoming one another as Christ welcomes each one of us (cf. Romans 15:7). As St. Cyprian has written, "The kingdom of God means Christ himself."

Let us daily turn to Christ, the Word made flesh who dwells among us so that his bud may blossom within us, bearing fruit that fills the earth with knowledge of the Lord, as water covers the sea (cf. Isaiah 11:1-2).

Then justice and peace shall flower for ever. ❧

# Perfection

Each and every human being is called to be holy, to be perfect (cf. Leviticus 19:2). After all, we are created in the image of God, who is holy and perfect (cf. Matthew 5:48).

Impossible?

Difficult, yes, but not impossible, and it is not more difficult than the abundant assistance granted to us through Christ, through whom we can do all things (cf. Philippians 4:13). Superhuman strength is not required, only the will to turn away from the wisdom of this world.

The wisdom of this world tells us to look out for "Number One," to exact "an eye for an eye and a tooth for a tooth," to never give or do more than what is necessary. This is all foolishness in the eyes of God (cf. 1 Corinthians 3:19) because it never ends there. Violence begets violence.

God's wisdom reverses the tide. Take no revenge, the Book of Leviticus tells us (19:18). In Matthew's Gospel (5:38-48), Jesus says precisely the same thing. A cutting remark answered with another quickly spirals into an argument—or worse. Grudges and acts of selfishness have similar capacities to build upon one another. However, when such acts are met with gentle yet firm kindness, mercy, and generosity, our "enemies" are taken aback. Love is given the space to take root and grow in the foolish light of the Cross, which reconciled us to God while we were still enemies (Romans 5:8-10).

God's grace provides the strength to go the extra mile. Perfection is reached one step at a time on the path of holiness, and it all begins within each heart God has fashioned in his image. Love begets love.

# Here's Looking at You

Take a good look at John 1:35-42 . . . Now, notice anything? Doesn't it seem like there's a lot of *looking* going on in this Gospel passage?

John *watched* Jesus walk by.

*Look!* It's the Lamb of God, John says.

Jesus turned and *saw* John's disciples following him.

What are you *looking* for? Jesus asks.

Come and *see*, Jesus says when they ask where he's staying.

They went and *saw* where Jesus was staying.

Finally, when Andrew brings along his brother Simon, Jesus *looked* at him before identifying him and giving him the new name Peter. A little later, after Jesus calls Philip, and Philip, in turn, fetches Nathaniel with the words "come and *see*," Jesus tells Nathaniel he has known him all along: "I *saw* you under the fig tree [signifying messianic peace] before Philip called you" (John 1:48).

Isn't that interesting? So, what does it all mean? It means that God knows precisely who you are. He knows you better than you know yourself. His gaze on you is never diverted elsewhere, and it is not a gaze of harsh condemnation but one of tender compassion and love, for "I am gentle and humble in heart" (Matthew 11:29). God *looks* at us, *loves* us (cf. Mark 10:21), and invites us to follow him. There is no coercion involved. "Come and see," he says, almost playfully.

If we are truly looking for him, listening for him—in prayer, Scripture, the life of the Church, our relationships, our work, our everyday encounters, sorrows and joys, successes and failures, illness and health—we will find the Messiah as Andrew, Peter, Philip, and Nathaniel did. Even when we are *not* looking or listening, Jesus walks by, turns and sees us, and continually invites us: "Come and see." He knows us, comes to meet us where we are, and then beckons us to follow him to where he is, to whom we belong—to become who we are called to be.

A sense of divine familiarity pervades much of Scripture. In the Old Testament, the boy Samuel "did not yet know the Lord," yet God called out to him as he slept, waiting patiently for him to respond, "Speak, for your servant is listening" (1 Samuel 3:3b-10, 19). Though Samuel up to that point knew nothing of the Lord, God knew him through and through and called out to him. Likewise, St. Paul reminds us that our *bodies* are members of Christ, that we are *joined* to the Lord and are one in Spirit with him. "Your bodies are members of Christ," he says. "Your body is a temple of the Holy Spirit within you, which you have from God. . . . You are not your own" (1 Corinthians 6:15, 19).

*We belong to God*, who is intimately familiar with us. As the psalmist prays:

> O Lord, you have searched me and known me. You know when I sit down and when I rise up; you discern my thoughts from far away. You search out my path and my lying down, and are acquainted with all my ways. Even before a word is on my tongue, O Lord, you know it completely. For it was you who formed my inward parts; you knit me together in my mother's womb. Your eyes beheld my unformed substance. In your book were written all the days that were formed for me, when none of them as yet existed (Psalm 139:1-4, 13, 16).

This is a message today's world needs to hear, to believe, to *live*. Each of us, in our own way, typically molds an image of who we *think* we are, who *others* think we are. We struggle daily to live up to such "false idols." God calls us gently away from our own ideas and notions. In revealing himself to us, he shows each and every one of us who we *really* are, who we are meant to be, who we can become. Like with Simon Peter, God calls us to follow him, to glorify God in our bodies, and take on a new identity in Christ—while still remaining ourselves. In Christ, we are transformed into our true identity.

Peter did not change instantly. Under the gaze of God, he remained a deeply flawed man. But he had discovered Christ, and his potential self in Christ, and he was willing to follow him. He was on the way. So it is with each one of us.

Jesus sees you, knows you.

"What are you looking for?" he asks. "Come and see who you will become through me." ♣

# Come as You Are, But Change

What should I wear? It's one of the first questions we excitedly ask ourselves when we receive an invitation of some sort. It's not a frivolous question. A tuxedo would be out of place at a backyard barbecue, and shorts and sandals would be inappropriate for a wedding. Likewise, business attire is expected for those called to company meetings, but old jeans and a t-shirt are more suitable for a friend's invitation to a painting party.

Most of these cultural expectations persist, though in recent years the boundaries may have become a bit blurry. How we dress for an important function (formal or informal) to which we've been invited says something about our degree of receptiveness, gratitude, and respect for the host and other guests. And it's not always easy. I'm the first to admit that I'm much more comfortable in backyard-barbeque and painting-party apparel! Fortunately for me and those who have to look at me, my Benedictine habit "cleans me up" a bit!

Jesus, as he so often does, instructs through a parable in Matthew 22:1-14, comparing the Kingdom of Heaven with a wedding feast. It must be kept in mind that he speaks these words to the chief priests and elders of his own time, who did not exactly meet with his approval. However, the message of the parable is no less urgent for us in the Church today. Clearly, the king in the parable is God, and the son is Jesus. The king plans a great wedding feast for his son, and invites many guests. "Everything is ready; come to the wedding banquet," he says.

But the invited guests refuse to come, ignore the invitation to attend to "more important things," or even worse, mistreat and kill the messengers bearing the invitation. There are many in today's world, and in ages past, who have responded in such ways to God's generous invitation to the banquet of grace, mercy, and peace. Because of their own refusal, they are deemed unworthy of the Kingdom of God. It is a personal choice.

But some *do* come. Some accept the invitation, and *all* of these are welcomed. As Matthew's Gospel states, when those first invited failed to show up, the king's servants "went out into the streets and gathered all whom they found, *both good and bad.*" This is the Church's invitation to us all. The Church—particularly through the Eucharist—prefigures (albeit imperfectly in its human members) the heavenly banquet to which we are all invited. No one is to be excluded.

The Church's role is to gather all she finds, *both good and bad*, for the banquet of grace, mercy, and peace. We are the king's servants sent out to fill the hall with guests, and we *also* are the guests gathered in by the king's servants.

However, though the invitation is open to all, *both good and bad*, we must dress for the occasion. We need to ask ourselves, "What should I wear?" Being invited and accepting the invitation is *not enough*. We must have the proper degree of receptiveness, gratitude, and respect for the most gracious invitation we have received. As Matthew 22:14 states, "Many are called, but few are chosen." The Church invites all, but entrance into the Heavenly Kingdom and full participation in the Wedding Banquet of the Lamb requires a lifelong, full-hearted response. The "chosen" are the ones who *choose* to do this of their own free will.

In this Gospel passage, the king encounters a guest not dressed in a wedding garment, the appropriate attire for the occasion. Yes, the guest *had been* invited, but his response to the invitation was not full. It was half-hearted. In essence, he "chose" to be cast out.

Jesus was speaking allegorically. The issue at stake is obviously not about clothing. What Jesus persists in telling us throughout all the gospels is that while *all* are invited to God's feast—*both good and bad*—in order to be truly "chosen," we must genuinely express the proper degree of receptiveness, gratitude, and respect. The Church is to welcome all, but there *will* be a Last Judgment for each one of its members. What we are "wearing" at that moment will matter enormously.

Jesus insists on reminding us of this reality. For example, in Matthew 13:47-48, Jesus says, "The Kingdom of Heaven is like a net that was thrown into the sea and caught fish of every kind; when it was full, they drew it ashore, sat down, put the good into baskets but threw out the bad." Elsewhere, he speaks of separating the wheat from the weeds, the sheep from the goats—not now, but at the Last Judgment. Until then, the guests are allowed to mingle with one another at the banquet provided by the Church.

The point is this: Mere church membership, lackadaisical observance, and doing only what is necessary to fulfill minimum requirements are not guarantees of entrance into the Kingdom of Heaven at the Last Judgment. We must have on our wedding garments. We must respond faithfully throughout our lives—in every aspect of our lives—to something very specific.

This is no esoteric formula beyond our reach. In the Gospel of John, as Jesus begins his ministry at the wedding at Cana, Mary (representing the Church) says to the servants (us): "Do whatever he [Jesus] tells you" (John 2:5).

And what does Jesus tell us to do? In the Gospel of Luke (10:25-28), a scholar of the law asks Jesus directly: "What must I do to inherit eternal life?" Jesus responds with a question, implying that the scholar already knows the answer: "What is written in the law?" And the scholar replies: "You shall love the Lord your God, with all your heart, and with all your soul, and with all your strength, and with all your mind; and your neighbor as yourself." Jesus tells him: "You have given the right answer; *do* this and you will live."

This is what we must wear as God's invited guests to the banquet of grace, mercy, and peace. We must put on the wedding garment of pure and total love of God, and our neighbor as ourselves. St. Paul elaborates: "As God's chosen ones, holy and beloved, *clothe yourselves* with compassion, kindness, humility, meekness, and patience. Bear with one another and, if anyone has a complaint against another, forgive each other; just as the Lord has forgiven you, so you also must forgive. Above all, *clothe yourselves* with love, which binds everything together in perfect harmony" (Colossians 3:12-14).

It is a simple command, but not an easy one to carry out. This wedding garment chafes a little at first. Like a pair of new shoes, it takes a while to wear it in. The good news is that we don't have to do it all alone. This is why God *gives* us the Church, the Eucharist and other sacraments, Scripture, public worship and private prayer, the ability to perform good works, and faith. These are not gifts we give to God, but things God *gives to us* for our benefit, for our being built up for the Kingdom.

As St. Paul says in Philippians 4:19: "God will fully satisfy every need of yours according to his riches in glory in Christ Jesus." In other words, *come to the feast*, and *Christ himself will hand you the wedding garment* to put on as you enter the banquet hall.

With the help of Christ the bridegroom, we all "clean up pretty nice," both good and bad. We can come as we are, but must change. If we so choose. ♣

# Give Me This Water

"I am thirsty," Jesus said from the cross (John 19:28). The Son of God thirsts for our faith in him, our conversion, and our eternal union in the Holy Trinity. And to prove it, as St. Paul says, he died for us *while we were still sinners* (Romans 5:1-2, 5-8).

For this reason, in John's Gospel (4:5-42), Jesus says to the Samaritan woman—who is a foreigner in a hostile region and a sinner—"Give me a drink." She has come to the deep, dark well to draw stagnant water because it's all she knows. Yet, hidden in her heart is a thirst for something more life-giving, and Jesus patiently draws that holy desire out of her. He slowly and lovingly turns her toward conversion by offering her "living water."

However, the Gospel passage is not about water, but rather life in Spirit and truth that Jesus offers to us all. Later in John's Gospel, Jesus extends this invitation: "Let anyone who is thirsty come to me, and let the one who believes in me drink. As Scripture has said, 'Out of the believer's heart shall flow rivers of living water'" (John 7:37-38).

Without water for our bodies, we die. And without the living water of the Spirit, our souls remain submerged in the Samaritan woman's deep, dark well of lifeless water. However, Jesus does not force our hand. He engages the woman on her terms. He allows her to direct the flow of the conversation. So he does with us.

Gradually, the woman at the well begins to trust him, and finally says to him, "Give me this water." The moment for her conversion has arrived, but Jesus does not condemn. Again, he slowly and lovingly states the facts, and then allows her to absorb and respond to them at her own pace.

The Samaritan woman prefigures the Church. Just as Isaac, Jacob, and Moses met their wives at a well, Christ engages his Bride (the Church, and our individual souls), and offers us his life-giving Spirit.

Just as with the Samaritan woman, Jesus is patient and loving with us. His hope is that finally, like her, we will believe, leave behind our old water jar (way of life), and pick up a new vessel that pours his Spirit into the lives of others.

He alone satisfies our thirst for eternal life. Let us ask him, "Give me this water." ♠

# Exposed by the Light

In addition to the story of the Samaritan woman at the well (John 4:5-42), John's Gospel includes another lengthy, intriguing, and exceedingly rich passage (9:1-41) focusing on our call to conversion in Christ. With the Samaritan woman, the symbol of living water was employed to signify new life in Christ. In John's ninth chapter, it is primarily light—or more specifically, the gift of sight. (Incidentally, John heavily employs both metaphors—living water and light—throughout his Gospel.)

Just as with the Samaritan woman, the nameless blind man in John 9 is gradually drawn into a deeper recognition of Jesus' identity. As he is questioned about his newfound sight, he first refers to his healer as "the man called Jesus." Later, he calls him a prophet. Still later, he recognizes him as a man from God, and finally, after being excommunicated from temple worship, he converses with Jesus, confesses his faith in him, and calls him Lord.

Here, there is a progression of faith that is signified in a very visible way during the liturgy for the Easter Vigil each year. At that time, the Easter candle is lit from a fire outside the darkened church, and then leads us inside as we exclaim "The Light of Christ. *Thanks be to God.*" One flame gives light to all, and the church's interior is illuminated for the celebration of the Easter mysteries. Gradually, we are led into the light. Once in darkness, we have become children of light through Christ, the Light of the world. This is the Good News we celebrate each and every Sunday and proclaim each day throughout the year.

The Pharisees, on the other hand, are moving in the opposite direction. Arrogant in their own self-appointed light, they gradually move into the darkness, unable to see or believe in the true light of Christ. Ironically, having cast out the man who was blind, they become blind themselves and end up outside the illuminated church. Rather than rejoicing in the blind man's newfound gift of sight, they judge, condemn, and ridicule. They cannot see beyond appearances—their own preconceived notions of what constitutes true sanctity.

So, we in turn must ask ourselves daily: "Which direction am I headed?"

In the words of the priest as he lights the candle at the Easter Vigil: "May the light of Christ rising in glory dispel the darkness of our hearts and minds." ♠

# The Real Deal

J esus taught as "one having authority, and not as the scribes," we are told in Mark 1:21-28. He was authentic, the real deal, no question about it. The implication is that the scribes—the synagogue "authorities"—were *not* authentic. They may have been good people, and their teaching may have been correct, but their motives were suspect. They did not teach with valid authority.

In Deuteronomy 18:15-20, Moses relays God's message to the people that he will eventually send a prophet like Moses, one to whom they should listen. As we know from the Old Testament, many great prophets succeeded Moses, and they all prefigured the Great Prophet, who is Christ. However, there were also false prophets, Moses warns the people against them. Again, they may have been good people, and their teaching may have been correct, but their motives were suspect.

Even the most sincere among us must acknowledge that, as commentator Carroll Stuhlmueller, C.P., writes, we carry some "measure of dishonesty and bias, of partial blindness to the truth and favoritism toward our own insights and personal causes." Our motives, if we are completely honest with ourselves, our often suspect and driven by concern for self above all else. Even "good" people do the *right* things for the *wrong* reasons. As imperfect human beings, in a sense we *all* lack authenticity.

In his mercy, love, and compassion, God desires nothing more than to restore our authenticity—to reveal who we are truly meant to be as children created in his image. He does not wish us to be anxious, distracted, or divided by suspect motives—to be *false* selves. And so, as Deuteronomy prophesies, God raised up for us Jesus, the Great Prophet, from among us. He was flesh and blood like us, yet filled with the Spirit of God the Father, and this Spirit he breathes upon us, into us, casting out with authority all that is false and divisive.

In the passage from the first chapter of Mark's Gospel cited above, Jesus enters the synagogue, teaches with authority, and then encounters a man with an unclean spirit who recognizes who Jesus truly is. It is an important scene, setting the tone and direction for the entire Gospel.

Jesus the Great Prophet comes with the authority of God to save, heal, and restore. He enters the synagogue of our souls, and fills God's temple within us with the Holy Spirit. There he encounters our false selves, the divided heart guided by suspect motives. Then, with compassion for us, he condemns not the human being, but rebukes the evil spirit within: *"Be silent, and come out of him!"*

After being baptized, announcing that the Kingdom of God is at hand, and then calling his first disciples, these are the very first words of Jesus' public ministry. It is what he came to do. With authority, he drives out all that divides our souls, our selves, from their true dignity, ultimately heaping all that is false on his own shoulders and nailing it to the cross, where all division, anxiety, and distraction is defeated forever. And, in the hope of the Resurrection that is ours, he restores our true selves, our authenticity.

If we let him in, open our hearts to him, ask him to stay with us through the gifts of prayer, Scripture, the sacraments, the life of the Church, and the practice of virtue, then we can truly say as did St. Paul: "It is no longer I who live, but it is Christ who lives in me" (Galatians 2:20). If we listen to him as one having authority, then the unclean spirit within will obey and come out.

It may require a lifetime to align our motives with all our thoughts, words, and deeds in order to become our authentic selves in Christ through the love of God and his Holy Spirit. However, Jesus assures us that "I am with you always, to the end of the age" (Matthew 28:20).

In the end, as the "good thief" crucified with Jesus demonstrated (cf. Luke 23: 39-43), it is not perfection that counts, but *authenticity*. As St. John wrote, "If we say that we have no sin, we deceive ourselves, and the truth is not in us. If we confess our sins, he who is faithful and just will forgive us our sins and cleanse us from all unrighteousness" (1 John 1:8-9).

That, thanks be to God, is the real deal. ♠

# The Finger of God

"The Spirit is called the finger of God," said St. Gregory the Great. "When the Lord put his fingers into the ears of the deaf mute, he was opening the soul of man to faith through the gifts of the Holy Spirit" (cf. Mark 7:31-37). This was foretold by the prophet Isaiah (35:4-7a): "Here is your God . . . He will come and save you. Then the eyes of the blind shall be opened, and the ears of the deaf unstopped; then the lame shall leap like a deer, and the tongue of the speechless sing for joy."

Jesus' actions in the Gospel passage cited above, then, are signs that God's long-awaited promises of deliverance, redemption, and healing have been fulfilled in Jesus Christ, God's Word made flesh. However, we must look beyond Jesus' many acts of physical healing throughout the gospels for what they ultimately signify. They are signs of something much greater: "By freeing some individuals from the earthly evils of hunger, injustice, illness and death, Jesus performed messianic signs. Nevertheless, he did not come to abolish all evils here below, but to free men from the gravest slavery, sin, which thwarts them in their vocation as God's sons and causes all forms of human bondage" (*Cathechism of the Catholic Church*, 549).

And so, in Mark's Gospel, Jesus "took [the deaf mute] aside in private, away from the crowed." The afflicted man enters the presence of God's Word in silence and solitude, and only in that setting does he become able to hear and speak as one should. True deliverance, redemption, and healing from earthly evil are brought about by a personal encounter with Jesus Christ (often mediated by human disciples; as we hear in this Gospel passage, the deaf mute is brought by others to Jesus, and they beg Jesus to heal him; he does so, but only after leading him away from the crowd so they can be alone).

Religion is not merely moral instruction and doctrine. It is not about personal wealth and health. It is *certainly* not a political cause. At its heart, true religion is a relationship with the God who comes to save us. And he meets us in the silence of our hearts, which his fingers shaped from the beginning. ❧

# Turning the Wheel

"No man is an island," the poet John Donne observed. Similarly, Pope Emeritus Benedict XVI wrote: "No man is an island, entire of itself. Our lives are involved with one another; through innumerable interactions they are linked together. No one lives alone. No one sins alone. No one is saved alone."

In other words, we're all in this together. God is the Island, who draws us into the Divine Presence. As we draw near to God, we become closer to one another. Calling to mind an image employed by Abba Dorotheos of Gaza (a sixth century monk and hermit), imagine a large wheel with many spokes. God is the hub—or center—of the wheel, while each of us stands along the circumference. If we each turn toward God and move toward the hub along the spokes (let's say these represent Scripture, prayer, a life of faith, etc.), two things simultaneously occur as the spokes gradually converge on the hub. As we draw closer to God, we become closer to one another. And, as we become closer to one another, we become closer to God. Of course, the reverse is also true. The farther we travel away from God along a spoke, the farther we become from those on the other spokes.

As we know, drawing closer to one another is not so easy to accomplish in practice. People have difficulty being together at times—whether in a family, neighborhood, workplace, faith community, city, or country. We're all different, and we're all at different points on that wheel—if we're on it at all. The whole thing hinges, it seems, on *turning toward* God and genuinely *moving toward* God through Scripture, prayer, a life of faith, etc. The rest will take care of itself. We have difficulty doing this because at some point along our individual "spoke" or path to God, we tend to stall. "OK, that's far enough," we seem to say. We become our own little hub, unconnected with anything, really, and certainly not helping the overall wheel's design.

It's a great consolation (and a challenge) that the early Christians struggled with this as well. The New Testament letters are replete with descriptions of communities torn by all sorts of divisions and disputes. "Bear one another's burdens, and in this way you will fulfill the law of Christ," Paul admonishes the Galatians (6:2). "Bear with one another and, if anyone has a complaint against another, forgive each other; just as the Lord has forgiven you, so you also must forgive," the Letter to the Colossians reminds us (3:13).

We are to bear with and forgive one another. Jesus is pretty clear on that, too—many times over. Not easy, but true. If we truly take to heart what we've read or heard in Scripture, and then actually apply it to everyday situations and act on it, we will be closer both to God and to our neighbor. But if we stall along the spoke and become our own little hub, our own island, we will invariably be unconnected to either, and wobbling off course.

The key, as mentioned, is taking that first step—*turning toward God*, and then *moving forward*. It seems to get easier as long as we keep *moving*. Scripture provides the fuel for that motion. If we have the fuel (desire), the Holy Spirit will map out plenty of opportunities to keep the wheel of love turning around the Love of God. ♠

# God in the Moment

# High Noon

One day, while traveling in Switzerland a few years ago, I wandered into a shop in the city of Luzern to browse around. It was noon, and in the shop, I overhead a woman with a British accent ask the clerk a question:

"Are those bells ringing for some sort of service?" she asked, referring to the tolling coming from a church somewhere in the city.

"They're ringing because it's lunchtime," answered the clerk, hesitating.

The woman who asked the question laughed as if this were the funniest thing in the world. I will give her the benefit of the doubt and presume that it was nervous laughter at not having realized that it was noon. Surely, there are church bells that ring at noon where she is from.

Perhaps not, though. At Saint Meinrad Archabbey in southern Indiana, I have grown accustomed to bells marking the day, every 15 minutes, 24 hours a day, 7 days a week. I have helped ring them manually to summon worshippers to the church for the Liturgy of the Hours, Mass, solemn professions, ordinations, and funerals. And on ordinary days, they serve to remind me not only what time it is, but Whose time it is, and that we all live each moment in the presence of God Eternal (OK, on my *good* days).

For many people in the United States at least, hearing church bells tolling throughout the day for a Mass, wedding, or simply for "lunchtime" was part of daily living a generation or two ago. But it strikes me (pun intended) that the experience has become less common in recent years as the neighborhood church has slowly lost its place as the focal point of community life. Before coming to the monastery in 2006, I lived in a number of neighborhoods where church bells were only heard on Sunday morning.

In many European countries, it's quite the opposite. Whatever effect secularization has had on European society, the bells are loud and clear and quite numerous. I find it comforting (now). In Rome, it is not uncommon to hear church bells ringing somewhere in the city all day long. And in each town I visited in Europe during the summer of 2010 (I was in Switzerland, Italy, France, Germany, and Austria), church bells marked the time in prominent fashion for all the citizenry to hear. There were a number of occasions that summer when I stopped whatever I was doing and just quietly listened to the tolling, making it my prayer.

There are numerous bells at our mother abbey of Maria Einsiedeln in Switzerland—many more than at Saint Meinrad, which has six. So many of the bells ring at so many different times of the day at Einsiedeln, that sometimes I was not quite sure what they were signaling. However, when the largest of the bells (which weighs nearly seven tons and is more than 400 years old) sounds, it's for something important. For one thing, it rings at noon every Friday. Yes, that is lunchtime. But before lunch, the monks gather in church to pray. And the largest bell rings at noon every Friday for one very specific reason—it is the hour and day the Church has traditionally recalled Christ's crucifixion for the life of the world.

It is a moment of gratuitous eternity, and that is something for which we can all be thankful—and for lunch, too. ♠

# Redeeming the Time

"I am the way, and the truth, and the life," Jesus says in John 14:6. "No one comes to the Father except through me." These words have deep and dire implications for the manner in which we disciples are called to live each moment of every day.

Jesus was not merely an ancient sage and miracle-worker. At this *very moment*, he is God among us (Emmanuel) in the flesh, which he offered on the altar of the Cross for the life of each individual soul throughout time.

How so? The answer that Jesus himself provides scandalized many of his followers, leading them to turn away from him; to this day, it remains offensive and incomprehensible to many. But it is the "source and summit of the Christian life" (*Lumen Gentium*, 51), both the wellspring and goal of God's grace, because it is Christ himself, who is the way and the truth and the life—the answer that it is the *Eucharist* that makes us tick, and Jesus puts it quite firmly:

> Unless you eat the flesh of the Son of Man and drink his blood, you have no life in you. Those who eat my flesh and drink my blood have eternal life, and I will raise them up on the last day; for my flesh is true food and my blood is true drink. Those who eat my flesh and drink my blood abide in me, and I in them. Just as the living Father sent me, and I have life because of the Father, so whoever eats me will live because of me" (John 6:53-57).

Eating and drinking each day, several times a day, sustains life for our mortal bodies. If we don't eat or get proper nourishment, we die. And even if we do eat properly, we still eventually die. By contrast, Jesus says, "I am the living bread that came down from heaven. Whoever eats of this bread will live forever; and the bread that I will give for the life of the world is my flesh" (John 6:51). Here, Jesus reasserts the connection between time and eternity that had been splintered in the Garden of Eden. Eating from the tree of the knowledge of good and evil that led to death gives way to eating from the Tree of Life so that we "may have life, and have it abundantly," as Jesus says (John 10:10).

Because of the first act, by which, to our detriment, we chose our own will (earthly food) over the will of the Father (heavenly food), God himself, in the Second Person of the Holy Trinity, gives his flesh for the life of the world on the Cross—heavenly food under the species of earthly food. God became human so that humanity might become God, to share eternal life with its Creator—beginning right now in our earthly lives. "Now is the day of salvation" (2 Corinthians 6:2). In this way, the full purpose of the Incarnation is revealed. "As all die in Adam, so all will be made alive in Christ," as St. Paul says (1 Corinthians 15:22).

In other words, in Christ, Eternal Divinity redeems human time. God becomes part of it, and it a part of him, to point it toward heaven. In the Eucharist, Christ becomes our spiritual food in the form of earthly bread and wine so that we who are broken may be made whole, and then, in turn, share ourselves as his Body for the life of the world. It is the principal means by which Christ dwells among us—as the mystical Body of Christ.

This is why St. Paul tells the Ephesians that they should be "making the most of the time" (Ephesians 5:16). However, translations such as the *Douay-Rheims* and *King James Version* have "redeeming the time." Those words add another dimension of understanding. In this sense, to "redeem" means to purchase something (or someone) in order to remove the object or person from current circumstances and offer freedom. In this way, Christ redeems us from sin, purchasing our freedom from slavery to corruption, with his own life-giving life. And "time" here does not mean, "We have plenty of time before dinner," but rather, "It's time for dinner!" It means *now*—a point in time, the moment of decision, a window of opportunity that is about to close. It means the train leaves the station promptly at 7:30 a.m., and if you're not on it, you will not get to where you'd like to go.

The entire sentence in this passage from Ephesians is this: "Be careful then how you live, not as unwise people but as wise, making the most of the time [or, 'redeeming the time'), because the days are evil" (Ephesians 5:15-16). The last phrase, "because the days are evil," is the key to it all. By our own lives, nourished and sustained by Christ, who gave *his* life for the world, we are to live accordingly and thereby "purchase" the current moment from the grip of evil. "Do not be foolish, but understand what the will of the Lord is," St. Paul continues (5:17).

So "making the most of the time" means much more than living life to the fullest and grabbing all the gusto one can muster. It means striving to do God's will at every turn, at each and every moment. "Redeeming the time," St. Augustine says, "means sacrificing, when the need arises, present interests in favor of eternal ones, thereby purchasing eternity with the coin of time."

It means that as Eucharistic people, we must rescue our everyday lives from the pattern that has been set by that bite of disobedience in the Garden of Eden. We, as Body of Christ, must transform the tree of the knowledge of good and evil, from which our parents brazenly dared to snatch equality with God, into the Tree of Life, from which Christ feeds the world.

It is a matter of life and death, and there is no time to waste.

# "*Maranatha*"
## ("Come Lord")

When the First Sunday of Advent rolls around each year, it seems that much of our consumer society has already been celebrating the "holiday season" for weeks. But not us—not yet. Instead, we are told: "Keep awake! Be ready. The Son of Man is coming at an unexpected hour."

How do we prepare for the unexpected? Perhaps the answer is simpler than it seems. When we are expecting a special guest to come into our home, we usually know the approximate hour, but our true focus is really not on the time of the guest's arrival. Rather, it is on being fully present to that guest whenever he or she arrives. We want the guest to feel welcome, comfortable, at home.

As Christians, we believe Jesus already dwells among us—in Word and Sacrament, and in the life of the Church of which we are members. But are *we* present? Have we, as St. Paul says, "put on the Lord Jesus Christ" (cf. Romans 13:11-14) and made him at home within us? Are we attentive to the moments and circumstances into which the unexpected light of the Lord is born?

The annual celebration of Advent—which means "Coming"—invites us to become increasingly present to the arrival of our Savior *each* and *every* day of our lives. By preparing for his coming year after year, we prepare for the Final Coming of Christ—that hour that encompasses all eternity.

Let us, then, be present *this* moment, for our "salvation is nearer to us *now* than when we became believers" (Romans 13:11). ♣

# Incarnate Vigilance

The theme of the Christian's need for vigilance or watchfulness is clear enough in our celebration of the season of Advent, when we quietly await the coming of Christ in a deeper manner. However, there is something more at stake than merely anticipating either the birth of Christ or the end time and final coming of Christ. That is not good enough, as the Gospel parable of the 10 virgins in a wedding party demonstrates (Matthew 25:1-13). All 10 kept vigil, but only five entered the wedding feast of the bridegroom (Christ).

Phrases throughout much of Scripture (see also Wisdom 6:12-16 and 1 Thessalonians 4:13-18) exhort us to keep vigil, be aware, and stay awake. But since we, the Church, are the virgins awaiting Christ the Bridegroom, we must also be prepared. We can't simply wait. Being *vigilant* also means being attentive to our day-to-day reality—yet always from an eternal perspective.

Whether we acknowledge it or not, we participate (positively or negatively) in spiritual realities that extend infinitely beyond the visible world. We participate in those realities not merely when we die or when Christ comes. We do so *here* and *now*. Each moment in time has eternal significance for each one of us—as individuals and as collective humanity. As the New Testament authors tell us, we must work out our salvation (cf. Philippians 2:12), not merely wait for it. "Faith without works is dead" (James 2:26).

Being vigilant means working out our salvation through the good works that come from God as a result of our faith. As the Letter to the Ephesians states: "By grace you have been saved through faith, and this is not your own doing; it is the gift of God—not the result of works, so that no one may boast. For we are what he has made us, *created in Christ Jesus for good works, which God prepared beforehand to be our way of life* (Ephesians 2:8-10).

This is why the Incarnation which we commemorate each year is so central not only to our Advent and Christmas celebrations, but throughout the year. Each liturgical year, we return full-circle to recall and be renewed by this mystery of our faith.

Like the 10 virgins, we as Christians hold lamps in hopeful expectation of the coming of the Bridegroom. These lamps—our good works—are meant to bring the light of Christ into the world for all to see. We are the light of the world, Jesus tells us (Matthew 5:14). Our good works—praising and thanking God, feeding the hungry, sheltering the homeless, visiting the sick, counseling and instructing in the ways of the Gospel, forgiving offenses, praying for the living and the dead, etc.—bring Christ to life and impart his saving grace here and now.

However, these lamps of good works must have oil. They must be fueled with "little drops of love," as Blessed Mother Teresa said. We cannot keep watch and light the way in hopeful expectation without the oil of love. Five of the 10 virgins forgot this, and were shut out of the Kingdom as a result!

There is yet a third element required to light the oil of *love* within the lamps of good works which are performed in *hope* as we await the arrival of the Bridegroom. We need the divine spark of *faith* that comes from God alone to make us glow and burn brightly. And here is where vigilance takes on a very interior nature which goes beyond mere exterior waiting. We must keep vigil within our very hearts—seek Wisdom, as we are urged in the passage from the book of that name cited above. In this passage, and throughout much of Scripture (Proverbs, Wisdom, Sirach), wisdom personified is identified with the Holy Spirit (cf. Wisdom 8:2-4; 9:17-18).

It is Wisdom—the Holy Spirit—that gives us light and life in Christ, that keeps our lamps of good works burning brightly. "Receive the Holy Spirit," Jesus tells us (John 20:22). "I am with you always, to the end of the age" (Matthew 28:20). This same Spirit was bestowed on us in Baptism and is made present in all the sacraments. We are sealed with Wisdom, and then reignited by Wisdom in our common worship, Scripture, and in prayer deep within our hearts.

And it is only with this Wisdom, visited upon us through the divine spark of *faith*, that we can light our lamps of *hope* with the oil of *love* and truly keep vigil for the coming of Christ. With Wisdom, we look forward to eternity with each and every moment of our day-to-day lives. With Wisdom, we work out our own salvation while doing what Jesus commands us: "make disciples of all nations, baptizing them in the name of the Father, and of the Son and of the Holy Spirit, and teaching them to obey everything that I have commanded you" (Matthew 28:19-20).

Vigilance means not only waiting for Christ, but making him present now. Then, with Wisdom at our side, like the five wise virgins, we will go into the wedding feast of the Bridegroom, where we shall always be with the Lord—who, through Wisdom, has been with us all along. ♣

# Where's the Fire?

Walking along the road to Emmaus, two of Jesus' disciples are disheartened. They still do not understand what it all means—Jesus' life, death, and resurrection. All their hope seems to have vanished along with him (see Luke 24:13-35).

Then Jesus himself joins them, and still, they do not truly see—at least initially. As Luke's Gospel tells us: "Jesus himself came near and went with them, but their eyes were kept from recognizing him."

Sadly, this is all too descriptive of many Christians. Jesus draws near, he walks with us, and tries to show us the way. If we allow him, as the two disciples do in today's Gospel, he will eventually get through in Word and Sacrament.

But how often do we really do that? So often, it seems to me, we are so intent on our routines, so "busy" with "important" matters, so eager to keep moving along to the next thing, that we leave Jesus there by the side of the road without even noticing him.

I can just imagine him calling out, "Hey guys, wait up!"

*Sorry*, we say politely, *we're late. We need to be going.*

Or, even if we do allow him to join us, doesn't it seem that all too often, we're not really "there"? Preoccupied, we just go through the motions—even in the breaking of the bread.

*First we do this, then that. Later comes this, that, and the other. We need to hurry, though.*

But, what if we simply slowed down a little, and . . .

. . . breathed deeply,

. . . allowed a little variation in the routine,

. . . entered into the sound of the gently falling rain and distant thunder,

. . . watched the evening sun sink beyond the horizon,

. . . read something without expecting to "get something out of it" or "do something with it"?

What if we noticed the journey rather than focusing on the destination?

What if we observed something without instantly analyzing or critiquing it?

What if we really listened to someone—anyone—without at the same time formulating our own judgment, response, or opinion?

What if we were simply present to the presence of Christ—God among us?

What if we just stood still to let Jesus catch up with us?

What else is so important, anyway?

Yes, as human beings, we need to be fruitfully occupied. But even noble or holy tasks can become ruthless masters. Life is not a series of tasks to be completed or appointments to be kept. Rather, life is about who we *bring* to those tasks and appointments—and who we *leave* with as we move from one to another. Hopefully, by the grace of God, who we bring and who we leave with is not quite the same person. There should be a discernible progression. We should become more like Christ—our companion along the Way. And that means spending time with him, for absolutely no other reason than because he is Jesus. Can we allow ourselves to simply "waste time" in the presence of Jesus each day?

Earlier in Luke's Gospel (10:38-42), Jesus tells the agitated Martha that her attentive sister Mary has chosen the better part. If Martha and Mary had been the two disciples on the road to Emmaus, I imagine Martha would be way out in front of Mary, worried about keeping good time, hollering back at her loitering sister to step it up.

Mary, meanwhile, would be wandering from one side of the path to another, absorbing the wonder of God's creation all around her. Stopping to watch a butterfly or pick a flower, perhaps, suddenly Jesus would be there. They then walk side by side, leisurely but passionately conversing, totally absorbed in one another, and calling out to Martha, "Hey, wait up!"

Martha, though, simply mutters and quickens her pace.

When I happen to notice Martha in another person, or in myself, I can only pray that our hearts will burn within us (cf. Psalm 39:4; Luke 24:32) for the presence of Christ. May it always be, so that as Jesus draws near and walks with us, our eyes recognize him, and our voices plead, "Stay with us, Lord!" 🌿

# The Middle Way

The middle is a tough place to be sometimes. Middle child. Mid-life. Mid-level management. Here, but not *there*. And here *we* are—seemingly caught in the middle, not quite there yet. In terms of our Christian faith, the promise has been made to us in Christ. But it has not yet been fully realized, so we must be patient, as the Letter of St. James says (5:7-10). This tension is inherent in many aspects of our lives, as it has been for people of all ages.

Hope is ultimately what sustains us on this journey, the prophet Isaiah reminds us (35:1-6a, 10). As God's people, we are a *pilgrim* Church—on the way, but not quite there. The ancient Israelites wandered in the desert for 40 years after Moses led them out of Egypt. The people of Isaiah's day longed for a return to Jerusalem during the Babylonian exile. The Letter of St. James was written after the time of Christ in the early days of the Church, when the Second Coming was expected at any moment.

Two thousand years later, we are still waiting.

Even John the Baptist asks Jesus: "Are you the one who is to come?" (Matthew 11:2-11).

Jesus' reply points to the works he is accomplishing that fulfill Isaiah's prophecy. He is a healing, suffering Messiah, whereas the world expects a fiery, powerful messiah. His message is that we should never let our expectations stand in the way of hope. God's ways are not ours.

And the good news is that Jesus *already* dwells among us: "I am with you always," he tells us (Matthew 28:20).

How? In prayer, Scripture, in the life of the Church and its members who comprise the Body of Christ, and in the sacraments—particularly the celebration of the Eucharist. He meets us along the way as we journey toward eternal union with God.

Perhaps the middle is not such a bad place to be after all. Ancient philosophers from Aristotle to St. Thomas Aquinas taught that virtue stands in the middle course. To borrow a phrase from the lyrics of the country music song "Meet in the Middle" by Diamond Rio, "We gain a lot of ground when we all give a little. There's no road too long when we meet in the middle."

May we meet Christ today in the midst of hardship, fear, and sorrow, so that with joy we may herald his coming each day as a New Advent! ♣

# The Circle of Life

Grace builds on nature. Holiness emerges through the ordinary. God's coming among us in the person of Jesus means that we don't have to stretch and strain toward the heavens. God is to be found in everyday life—especially within the family circle which radiates out from the center of our culture.

Our relationships with one another must be an expression of our relationship with God, particularly in the context of family life. In his letter to the Colossians (3:12-21), St. Paul offers us a simple set of qualities we must adopt for daily living as God's family:

Compassion

Kindness

Humility

Meekness (or gentleness)

Patience

Forbearance

Forgiveness

Love

Peace

Gratitude

Praise and worship of our God in all that we do or say.

The Holy Family of Jesus, Mary, and Joseph is our model, and through Christ—fully human and fully divine—we have become part of it. Let us live as "God's chosen ones, holy and beloved," each one of our days.

# Lost and Found

One thing that is striking about much of Scripture is the emphasis on God's initiative in seeking *us* (cf. Ezekiel 34:11-12, 15-17 and Matthew 25:31-46). Those who are serious about the spiritual life are often in danger of straining to direct it, thereby missing the obvious. If you've ever conducted a frantic 15-minute search for your car keys, only to realize they've been in your pocket (or your hand!) all along, you know what I mean.

We must seek God, but *true* seeking is not straining beyond our means. To seek involves standing still long enough to recognize what is right in front of us, as illustrated by the passage from Matthew's Gospel cited above. In the spiritual life, this means recognizing the presence of Christ in THIS moment, THIS person, THIS circumstance immediately before us. It means accepting God's message as it is presented to us so that we may do all for the sake of Christ, and "God may be all in all," as St. Paul says (1 Corinthians 15:28).

The point is that we really don't need to *seek* God as much as we must allow ourselves to be *found* by him. It is God who takes the initiative, as the passage from Ezekiel states: "I myself will search for my sheep, and will seek them out," says the Lord. No matter where we are or who we are, God comes among us to gather us to himself.

It is interesting to note the adjectives used to describe the sheep in the passage from Ezekiel. They are:

*Scattered*

*Lost*

*Strayed*

*Injured*

*Weak*

In one way or another, these words describe each one of us. But Christ the King and Good Shepherd comes to meet us (sometimes, seemingly, even as a sheep in wolf's clothing!) in our scattered, lost, strayed, injured, and weak existence. He becomes one with us in our humanity to lead us into the Eternal Kingdom and adorn us with the sparkling divinity befitting children of God. We don't attain heaven. It attains us—if we let it.

As we meditate on the glorious mystery of the Incarnation— God's supreme initiative in seeking out his lost sheep—we look to the King who comes not to rule and govern, but to love and guide us along the right way. As Pope Emeritus Benedict XVI remarked:

> By calling ourselves Christians, we label ourselves as followers of the King. God did not intend Israel to have a kingdom. The kingdom was a result of Israel's rebellion against God. The law was to be Israel's king, and through the law, God himself. God yielded to Israel's obstinacy and so devised a new kind of kingship for them. The King is Jesus; in him God entered humanity and espoused it to himself. God does not have a fixed plan that he must carry out; on the contrary, he has many different ways of finding man and even of turning his wrong ways into right ways. [We] are in the hands of the one who writes straight on crooked lines. ♠

# Small Wonder

It is odd, yet also fitting, that the joyful celebration of Christ's birth each year is followed so closely by the feast days (December 26 and 28) of St. Stephen, the first martyr, and the Holy Innocents. These gave their lives (the little ones unknowingly) so that Christ's Gospel might live and be proclaimed throughout the world, just as Jesus himself did. St. Stephen and the Holy Innocents, each in their own way, perpetuate Christ's eternal sacrifice, submitting to their persecutors so that Christ's light may live and grow in the hearts of all people.

As the French poet Charles Peguy recalled, in the case of the Holy Innocents, "They are the eternal imitations."

It may be rather easy to believe that a small child is closer to Christ than most of us who are more acquainted with the scars of sin and struggle. In the witness provided by care-free, yet totally dependent, youngsters, we are reminded that "unless you change and become like children, you will never enter the Kingdom of Heaven" (cf. Matthew 18:3; Mark 10:15).

However, more than sweet and simple innocence is involved here. Becoming like a little child means, as Jesus says, *changing*—turning our hearts to be completely dependent on, trustful of, and obedient to God. It means proclaiming the message of Christ's salvation in word and deed through self-sacrifice—whether martyrdom comes with swift and deadly blows or with the tiny, annoying pinpricks of daily life.

It also means that Christ speaks to us daily in the smallest of details, the most improbable (even painful) of events, and in the people many of us dismiss as not worth the effort or notice. Just as with the manger at Christmas, the empty tomb at Easter, or along the road to Emmaus after the Resurrection (cf. Luke 24:13-35), Christ lies hidden yet always present at the heart of our lives, waiting to be discovered by us with childlike wonder.

Most of all, it means that the power of sin and death which at every turn seeks to defeat Life itself *absolutely cannot win*. The destruction which evil inflicts before our eyes is ultimately its own undoing, all through the power hidden in childlike dependence on, trust in, and obedience to God. Pharaoh ordered that all newborn Hebrew boys be thrown into the Nile. Yet Moses—plucked from that same river—survived to lead his people out of Egyptian slavery. Hundreds of years later, Herod ordered the massacre of all newborn boys in the vicinity of Bethlehem. Yet the infant Jesus—escaping in the arms of Mary and Joseph—survived and emerged (again, from Egypt!) to save all people from slavery to sin by handing over his own life. Later, after Stephen was martyred, a fierce persecution of the first Christians was initiated in Jerusalem. People fled for their lives, but in the end, "those who were scattered went from place to place, proclaiming the word" (Acts. 8:4). The message of salvation cannot be thwarted, no matter what.

In all these instances, Life and Light ultimately prevail, as is the case today for those who believe. As St. John wrote, "the light shines in the darkness, and the darkness did not overcome it" (John 1:5). This light is none other than Jesus, who himself said, "I have come as light into the world, so that everyone who believes in me should not remain in the darkness" (John 12:46).

The pattern has been set, and the same event continues in each one of our lives to this very day. If we seek Christ, he will be found. If we ask, we will receive. And if we pick up our cross daily, follow him, and lose our lives for his sake, we will gain Life and Light itself.

Throughout it all, the Holy Innocents dance with delight around the Christ child. In harmony, the "eternal imitations" rejoice in the hope stored up in heaven for all who change and become like children. ❧

# Adventus

When the "holiday season" kicks off each year—around late November, if not before—much of the world makes a mad dash toward December 25. Along with ordinary tasks, the days are filled with decorating, buying, celebrating, buying, fretting, buying, baking, buying—in search of some nostalgic, yet vague sense of hope that, all too often, fails to satisfy and is kicked to the curb on Dec. 26.

By contrast, Christians (in theory, at least) profess this period as Advent (from the Latin term *adventus*, or coming).

Whose coming do we await? In faith, hope, and love, we await the coming of Christ—God among us—who comes to save humanity from the state that it has itself rendered. Jesus has come once to take on our humanity and redeem it. He will come again to fulfill God's promise and take all things to himself. And he is coming *now*, at this very moment—whatever season it is. Eternity will emerge from how we respond daily to God's eternal presence in the mystical Body of Christ.

Eternity will be what each of us makes of *today*.

While it's fine to engage in a little holiday cheer when the time comes, we do well to remember that Advent calls for a joyful *anticipation* of the Kingdom of God—yesterday, today, and forever. We must recall that the celebration of Christmas (which actually *begins* Dec. 25 and runs for many days thereafter) evokes that mystical event when God became man in the person of Jesus, whose name in Hebrew means "God saves." That should indeed bring us great joy—but not the fleeting, superficial, artificial joy so often peddled in the month of December. It is a *daily* joy tempered by the reality of the crucifixion, a wonderful paradox that gives rise to rejoicing with the psalmist: Lord, "there is forgiveness with you, so that you may be revered" (130:4).

Advent and Christmas, then, are solemn occasions steeped in true, everlasting joy as we await throughout all our days the full coming of the Kingdom of God. As author Alice Camille points out in her booklet *Waiting for God: The Grace of Advent*, there is more to it than a cute baby in a manger. It's serious business. Advent, she says, is a state of spiritual emergency.

Advent involves a different type of urgency than the festal fretting that so often surrounds us before Christmas even begins. We are reminded of this throughout the year at each Mass after the Lord's Prayer, when the priest says, "Deliver us, Lord, we pray, from every evil, graciously grant peace in our days, that by the help of your mercy, we may be always free from sin and safe from all distress, as we await the blessed hope and the coming of our Savior, Jesus Christ."

For the kingdom, the power, and the glory are yours now and forever. ♠

# Your Light Has Come

"Lift up your eyes and look around," the prophet Isaiah tells us (60:4). "Your light has come, and the glory of the Lord has risen upon you" (60:1). As people of faith, we must keep our gaze on heaven above but also "look around," to the circumstances and people on earth through whom the light of Christ shines. He is in each of us, all around us, yet we must *first* lift up our eyes, viewing everything from an *eternal* perspective that reveals God's immense love, mercy, and compassion.

Elsewhere, St. Paul tells us, "If you have been raised with Christ, seek the things that are above, where Christ is, seated at the right hand of God. Set your minds on things that are above, not on things that are on earth" (Colossians 3:1-2). As baptized Christians, we are raised with Christ in his baptism, on his Cross, and in his Resurrection. Raised with Christ in *this* light, God's glory shines upon us, and as Isaiah says, we then "shall see and be radiant; your heart shall thrill and rejoice" (60:5).

This is illustrated for us in the story of the magi from Matthew's Gospel (2:1-12). In Jerusalem, very near the town of Bethlehem where Christ is born, King Herod looks all around, but not above, and so is disturbed and frightened. The light of Christ is close by, but he cannot see it. On the other hand, the three magi from a distant land have their eyes uplifted to see Christ's star at its rising. So, they are impelled to look about for him, guided by the light above. They know who they are looking for, and in a spirit of humility, gratitude, and joy, they find him and give themselves to him by presenting their treasures.

The magi's encounter—God revealed to foreigners in a strange land through the newborn Christ—made them stewards of God's grace and co-partners in God's promise of eternal salvation revealed through the gospel. Herod, though a native of the land, remained disturbed. Fearfully looking around but without raising his eyes to heaven, he attempts to kill all the newborn children in Bethlehem to preserve his own treasures. In doing so, he remains in the dark, unable to see the light so visible to the magi from so far away—and eventually loses everything.

As we reflect on the mystery of what we term liturgically as the Epiphany—God's manifestation to *all* peoples through Christ's birth, his visit from the magi, his baptism, and his first miracle of changing water into wine at the wedding feast in Cana—we all do well to ask ourselves these questions:

*Are you greatly troubled?*

*Have you **first** raised your eyes to heaven?*

*Do you then look about the earth for the light of Christ with humility, gratitude and joy, eager to find him in the most unlikely of people and places, and offer there your greatest treasures?*

May our own encounter with Christ make each one of us radiant, our hearts thrilling and rejoicing with the gift of God's grace manifested to all the earth. Let us lift up our eyes to behold the Light of Christ. As we do, this light, this life, will be ours forever. Then, radiant with this light and life, we can look around and become beacons of hope for all around us who are disturbed and frightened. May we all become copartners in God's promise of eternal salvation revealed through the Gospel.

Your light has come, and the glory of the Lord has risen upon *you!* ❧

# Christian Life

# Fruit of the Vine

During the Liturgy of the Eucharist, at the Presentation and Preparation of the Gifts, the priest holds the chalice filled with wine and praises God with these words: "Blessed are you, Lord God of all creation, for through your goodness we have received the wine we offer you: fruit of the vine and work of human hands, it will become our spiritual drink." And the People of God respond, "Blessed be God, forever."

Since the priest is acting during the Mass *in persona Christi*, or in the person of Christ, this is a very profound mystery to consider. It is *together with Christ* that we offer the gifts we have received from God and praise the Father. It is a *participation* in the very life, death, and resurrection of Christ, so that we may go out and offer our very lives—*the work of human hands*. But at the same time, all we do, say, or think in the name of Christ is God-given grace, *the fruit of the vine*. All that is good which we offer to God was *first* given to us. Through Christ, we bear fruit for the Kingdom of God as stewards of the divine mysteries.

This theme is present throughout Scripture, but perhaps nowhere more explicitly than in John 15, when Jesus tells his disciples on the night he was betrayed: "I am the true vine, and my Father is the vinegrower. . . Abide in me as I abide in you. Just as the branch cannot bear fruit by itself unless it abides in the vine, neither can you unless you abide in me. I am the vine, you are the branches. Those who abide in me and I in them bear much fruit, because apart from me you can do nothing" (John 15:1, 4-5). The point is clear: we must remain connected to, or tapped into, the life-giving force (the "sap," as it were) of Christ the True Vine, to bear an abundant harvest of fruit—our good works—in building up the Kingdom of God, God's vineyard which he gives to us.

This vineyard image is common throughout Scripture (see, for example, Isaiah 5:1-7). In Matthew's Gospel (21:33-43), Jesus' parable of the landowner's vineyard and his wicket tenants serves as an allegory with several purposes: to confront the religious leaders of the time for being unfaithful stewards of God's grace, to point out the numerous prophetic voices they have ignored, to predict his own death as the fulfillment of these prophetic voices, and to foretell the fruition of the Church. You and I are the "other tenants" to whom the vineyard has now been leased by the owner of the vineyard, God the Father.

But we are not alone. The vine we tend as stewards *also tends us*. Christ joins us in the vineyard of the Church as the True Vine, giving us life so that we may, in turn, with him produce abundant fruit in praise of the Father—*the fruit of the vine and work of human hands*. In short, *it is Christ who gives life to the Church*. It is not a human institution, but was born on the cross, when water and blood—the very life of Jesus—poured out from his pierced side. Christ is our sap. And if we remain tapped into him through the Eucharist, in common worship, in prayer and Scripture, in the sacraments and tradition of the Church, we will bear his fruit as faithful tenants of the vineyard, saying with him, "Blessed be God forever."

The key to all this is expressed by St. Paul. "Do not worry about anything," he urges, "but in everything by prayer and supplication with thanksgiving let your requests be made known to God. And the peace of God, which surpasses all understanding, will guard your hearts and your minds in Christ Jesus" (Philippians 4:6-7).

Like the religious leaders in Jesus' day, we all have a tendency to beat down or "kill" the prophetic voices within and around us. It happens in numerous ways. Ignoring someone who clearly needs our help because we'd rather not bother, or because the person is someone we don't particularly like. Becoming so immersed in our outward activities that we squelch God's tiny whispering sound deep within and lose focus on what's really important in life. Worrying to the point of despair rather than trusting in God's providential care. There are myriad ways of disposing of prophetic voices sent by God to help us with care of the vineyard, his Church.

What St. Paul is saying is that through prayer and praise, we remain connected to Christ the True Vine. We participate in the mystery we contemplate. We listen to the prophetic voice of God deep within and around us. Our hearts and minds find the peace that the world cannot give. We bear abundant fruit—*fruit of the vine and work of human hands*—for the world to feast on and (hopefully) find peace as well.

But without Christ, we can do nothing. Before we can harvest the grapes, savor the wine, and pour it into the hearts of others, we must let the True Vine grow within us, give us life, and produce his abundant fruit.

Then, with the psalmist, we can say:

*What shall I return to the Lord*
*    for all his bounty to me?*
*I will lift up the cup of salvation*
*    and call on the name of the Lord.*
                    —Psalm 116:12-13

♠

# Scattered Seed

I n the opening verses of Scripture, God blesses humanity, saying, "Be fruitful and multiply" (Genesis 1:28). In the closing verses of the Bible, John is shown "the river of the water of life, bright as crystal, flowing from the throne of God and of the Lamb. On either side of the river is the tree of life with its twelve kinds of fruit, producing its fruit each month" (Revelation 22:1-2).

God calls us, his children, to be fruitful according to his Word—but not of our own accord. It is God's lavish generosity that plants, waters, warms, and produces the growth that leads to fruitfulness. As God says through the prophet Isaiah, "As the rain and the snow come down from heaven, and do not return there until they have watered the earth, making it bring forth and sprout, giving seed to the sower and bread to the eater, so shall my word be that goes out from my mouth; it shall not return to me empty, but it shall accomplish that which I purpose, and succeed in the thing for which I sent it" (55:10-11).

It may seem to us sometimes that God's graciousness is wasteful and foolish. The seed of his Word is scattered recklessly for all (cf. Matthew 13:1-23), but is often met with indifference, ignorance, opposition, and despair—both in the world and within our *own* hearts. As St. Paul says, "we know that the whole creation has been groaning in labor pains" (Romans 8:22).

However, marvelous effects result whenever *just a few* seeds are sown within receptive hearts. As Jesus says, "As for what was sown on good soil, this is the one who hears the word and understands it, who indeed bears fruit and yields, in one case a hundredfold, in another sixty, and in another thirty" God's generosity cannot be outdone. His Word, like the rain sent from the heavens to water the earth, *will* achieve its end far beyond our imagining.

Despite the barren, rocky, thorny terrain within and around us, those tiny seeds watered by heavenly dew will produce abundant, sweet fruit hanging from the branches of the tree of life in God's garden (cf. Revelation 2:7).

Let us taste and see!

# Out of the Depths

Whatever season we're in, we do well to recall that our faith should grow year-round, year by year, and that this faith involves *salvation* through Christ in *solidarity* and *service*. For example, when we emerge from the Christmas season and embark on ordinary time, the celebration of the Baptism of the Lord evokes a Christian sense of a New Year's resolution. However, just as with any resolution, its value is determined by how it's actually lived out—in this case, in the light of faith.

The prophet Isaiah (42:1-4, 6-7) depicts the ideal servant of God as one whose only purpose is to bring freedom and justice to all through self-sacrifice. In Matthew's Gospel (3:13-17), the voice from the heavens echoes that of Isaiah's prophecy as Jesus' mission is manifested at his baptism: "This is my Son, the Beloved, with whom I am well pleased." Jesus is the Servant sent into the world to redeem God's people.

Although he is without sin, Jesus is baptized to signify his solidarity with sinful humanity. Again, Isaiah and Matthew use similar terms. Isaiah speaks of God's servant freeing his people "from the dungeon," while Matthew says Jesus "came up from the water." In the ancient Hebrew worldview, just as suffering evoked sin, the deep waters of the sea suggested death. The "dungeon" of Sheol (hell) lurked below the seas, which sprung from the chaotic Abyss.

Scripture tells us, though, that God has power and authority over the waters, and therefore over sin and death. "In the beginning . . . the earth was a formless void and darkness covered the face of the deep, while a wind from God swept over the face of the waters. Then God said, 'Let there be light'" (Genesis 1:1-3). Much later, as the Israelites fled from the pursuing Egyptians, "Moses stretched out his hand over the sea. The Lord drove the sea back by a strong east wind all night, and turned the sea into dry land" (Exodus 14:21). Moses led God's people through the sea safely, and the waters returned to swallow up their enemies.

Psalm 107 offers thanksgiving to God for deliverance from trials, and verses 23-32 recount the joy of those whose lives were spared from the stormy waters: "Then they cried to the Lord in their trouble, and he brought them out from their distress; he made the storm be still, and the waves of the sea were hushed." Many of the psalms are filled with such images, and the gospels shed new light on them by recounting Jesus' ability to walk on water and calm stormy seas. Jesus, as Son and Servant of God, *conquers* and *transforms* sin and death. He makes "the depths of the sea a way for the redeemed to cross over" (Isaiah 51:10).

So, when Jesus is baptized, he is immersed in the depths of *our* darkness—filled with its sin, failure, disordered desire, pain, sorrow, and death. Then he arises, "the heavens were opened to him," and a voice from the heavens claims him as his Beloved Son. This, of course, prefigures Jesus' death and resurrection, and signifies God's plan of *salvation*. Jesus demonstrates his *solidarity* with us by entering into the Abyss with us and his *service* by bringing us into the Light with him.

If we are saved with him, we must also serve with him. So, we are reminded of our baptismal call as Christians—to bring freedom and justice to all through self-sacrifice.

No matter the season, that is by far the best resolution we can make—and then, by the grace of God, faithfully living it out. ♣

# Resounding on the Waters

One Fourth of July evening while on vacation, my brother-in-law carefully maneuvered his boat from the Ohio River onto the Muskingum and up into Marietta, Ohio. Anchored there with many other boaters as dusk fell, he and my sister, mother, nephew, and I prepared to watch the city's annual fireworks display over the water.

As the show began, it quickly became obvious that the only way to watch with ease was to recline on our backs or slouch down in our seats and look straight up into the starry sky. The shells were exploding directly over our heads, high above the river. Each soaring flare and burst of shimmering color was quickly followed by a splitting boom that seemed to slice the heavens and shake the mountains around us as if we were meeting God at the foot of Mount Sinai.

Positioned as we were, with our bodies parallel to the river and just a couple feet above the water, we also experienced an almost indescribable sensation. Each boom was quickly followed by a resounding echo that seemed to travel along the river and then back into our very bones through the water directly below us. If you've ever been on or near a lake or river during a thunderstorm or a fireworks display, you know what I mean. The water magnifies the sound descending from above.

The sensation reminded me of the theophany of Psalm 29, which describes the presence of God revealed in a thunderstorm over the water:

> *The voice of the Lord is over the waters;*
> *the God of glory thunders,*
> *the Lord, over the mighty waters.*
> *The voice of the Lord is powerful;*
> *the voice of the Lord is full of majesty.*

Some translations present the first line of this Psalm as "The Lord's voice *resounding* on the waters…," which for me seems quite vivid—like fireworks exploding over the water. Indeed, for those with ears to hear, the power and glory of God's word reverberates throughout human history.

Such imagery comes to mind while reflecting on the opening lines of Matthew 13:1-23. The text describes Jesus sitting down by the sea, and as large crowds gather around him, climbing into a boat and addressing the people standing along the shore. This is a perfectly practical act in and of itself. Jesus needed space from which to address his followers, and the water from which he spoke would have magnified his voice for all to hear.

However, there are deeper, theological implications as well. Imagine standing on that shore and listening to the power and force of Jesus' message being carried by the water directly into your bones. The Word made Flesh, God-Among-Us speaks, and the water magnifies the sound descending from above:

> The voice of the Lord is over the waters;
> > the God of glory thunders,
> > the Lord, over the mighty waters.
> The voice of the Lord is powerful;
> > the voice of the Lord is full of majesty.

From a boat used by human beings to sail across the water, the God of glory thunders, and his Word is magnified and carried throughout the world. This image, of course, can be connected with that of the story of creation in Genesis, in which the wind (or Spirit) of God sweeps over the waters (Genesis 1:1-2).

So what is being communicated to us through these passages from Holy Scripture? Perhaps the key to pondering this further lies in the next chapter of Matthew's Gospel—specifically Matthew 14:22-33—in which Peter is called forth by Jesus to walk on the water with him. Here we have the fearful disciples in a boat being tossed about by the waves on the stormy sea. Suddenly, Jesus appears, walking toward them on the water!

"Do not be afraid," Jesus tells them.

Then Peter expresses some measure of faith. "Lord, if it is you," he calls out, "command me to come to you on the water." A bold request! Jesus has no problem with it. "Come," he says.

So Peter gets out of the boat and begins to walk on the water toward Jesus. However, when he loses focus, he begins to sink and cries out for help. Jesus reaches out and saves him, and the wind dies down.

In the ancient world, the sea represented darkness, danger, and death. So, in a very real sense, these passages and images from Scripture illustrate God's redeeming power over these elements, manifested fully in the person of Jesus, which means "God saves."

However, God doesn't want us to simply listen to the message of salvation from the safety of the shore. Neither does he wish us to cower in fear as we are tossed about by life's storms. Jesus invites us to *step out of the boat*, to break out of our comfort zones and leave behind excessive concerns for health, wealth, control, and security.

He wants us to *participate* in his redeeming power over darkness, danger, and death. He desires for us to come to him, to magnify his voice, and carry his Word over the waters, echoing to the ends of the earth.

There is nothing to fear. If we begin to sink from time to time, he will be there to catch us. And we don't need to be as spectacular as a fireworks display. We simply need to walk with Jesus above the stormy waves and through the abyss, giving witness to the power of God that turns back the tide of darkness. In the words often attributed to St. Francis of Assisi: "Preach the Gospel. If necessary, use words."

God's voice can thunder through our lives if we allow his Word to travel through us like the Muskingum River carrying and magnifying the sound of booming fireworks descending from above. Mary, the mother of Jesus, is the perfect model in this regard. She doesn't say much in Scripture, but her witness to the Word born from her womb has echoed for 2,000 years. Her life, like the river during the fireworks show, magnifies God's voice for all to hear. "My soul magnifies the Lord," the pregnant Mary proclaims to Elizabeth (Luke 1:46) in the *Magnificat*, the canticle of praise the Church sings each evening at Vespers.

"Do not be afraid," Jesus says. "Come, and with the Spirit of truth and love . . . move on the water's face bearing the lamp of grace; now to all humankind let there be light" (a line from the hymn *God, Whose Almighty Word*, by John Marriott).

We are all called to be part of the show leading up to the grand finale! ♣

# Yes or No

The choice is ours. Drawing on God's commands to the Israelites as communicated by Moses (Deuteronomy 30:15-20), a passage from Sirach uses the word "choose" three times (Sirach 15:15-20). "Before each person are life and death, and whichever one chooses will be given," we are told. We are free to choose either good or evil, to trust in the ways of God or to trust in our own ways.

In Matthew's Gospel, Jesus emphasizes that he has not come to abolish the commandments given to the Israelites in the time of Moses, but to fulfill them—to deepen our understanding of them (Matthew 5:17-37). God's Word to us through the ages is made present to us in the person of Jesus. "I say to YOU" is a personal address by Jesus to each one of us.

His concern is that we live our lives by something more than merely observing rules of conduct or attempting to avoid breaking them. What counts is the *spirit* with which we do things. Love, after all, is a decision. It is *choosing* the good, *choosing* life.

When we do this, our eyes are opened more fully to the hidden wisdom of God (cf. 1 Corinthians 2:6-10) so that we can grow to maturity in the Spirit by following Christ.

May our "Yes" mean "Yes," and our "No" mean "No."

# Salt and Light

God's presence and power shine most brightly through human weakness. Cases in point: Sarah, Moses, Hannah, David, Isaiah, Peter, Paul, Augustine, Francis, Ignatius of Loyola, Thérèse of Lisieux, Mother Teresa, and many, many more throughout the course of salvation history.

When we are weak—not insincere or arrogant weakness, but truthful, humble weakness—then we are strong (cf. 2 Corinthians 12:10). Weakest—and strongest—of all is Christ, God made man, crucified as a common criminal as he saves us from our sins and defeats death.

With a true awareness of who we truly are before God, our light breaks through the darkness like the dawn; like a glowing, mountainside city in a dark countryside; like a lamp lit to illuminate a shadowy room, or like a stained glass window in a dim church (cf. Isaiah 58:8; Matthew 5:13-16). The point is this: human frailty does not prevent us from drawing closer to God. Rather, when it is freely acknowledged, it becomes the seasoning of our redemption, purifying and preserving us in the name of God.

When the light of the Gospel shines through our shortcomings, failures, and faults, we come to know that our faith rests not on human wisdom but on the power of God (cf. 1 Corinthians 2:5).

This is what it means to be the salt of the earth and the light of the world. ♣

# Piercing the Clouds

S ome of the descriptive words employed by Scripture's inspired authors in certain passages are telling in regard to humanity's never-ending struggles. For example, Sirach (35:12-22) speaks of the poor, the oppressed, orphan, and widow. St. Paul is imprisoned and knows that "the time of my departure has come" (2 Timothy 4:6-8, 16-18). He also is lonely—"All deserted me," he says. Meanwhile, in Luke's Gospel, the self-righteous Pharisee's prayer derides those whom he perceives as thieves, rogues, and adulterers (18:9-14).

Where do we see ourselves here in relation to God? In one way or another, and at one time or another, these terms describe many of us.

Whatever the case may be, the key to our approach to God lies not in perceived perfection, but in true humility. Our hope comes in the most unlikely of persons: in the passage from Luke's Gospel, Jesus points to the tax collector, considered at that time to be the most despicable of all human beings. There, in the corner of the Temple, he humbly acknowledges who he is and asks for God's merciful assistance. The tax collector—though far from perfect—recognizes his *need* for God, and so is justified in God's sight.

The self-righteous Pharisee, on the other hand, has done many commendable things, but takes credit for them all himself. He doesn't really *need* anyone, including God, in his mind. And so, Jesus says that it is the lowly tax collector (a sinner!), and *not* the haughty Pharisee (who did everything right!), whose prayer is heard. As Sirach points out, "the prayer of the humble pierces the clouds."

A truly humble person, the author of *The Cloud of Unknowing* said, "stands in the truth with a knowledge and appreciation for himself as he really is." When we approach God with that kind of transparency, as the tax collector does, the Lord stands by us and gives us strength— and the "crown of righteousness" awaits us no matter who we are.

Thanks be to God.

# Founded on Faith

Take *"these words of mine"* into your very being, Moses tells the ancient Israelites (Deuteronomy 11:18, 26-28, 32). Listen to *"these words of mine"* and act on them, Jesus tells the crowds (Matthew 7:21-27). It is no accident that this same phrase is used by both Moses—who prefigures Christ—and Jesus himself in addressing their followers. The same words address us today through Scripture. Jesus is the Word of God made flesh, and by giving us his very body and blood on the cross, his words become ours, and should become the very foundation of our daily lives.

In the Gospel passage, Jesus has just finished his Sermon on the Mount recorded in chapters 5-7 of Matthew (which, for all of us, are worth reviewing regularly). Concluding his discourse, he says, "Everyone then who hears these words of mine and acts on them will be like a wise man who built his house on rock. The rain fell, the floods came, and the winds blew and beat on that house, but it did not fall, because it had been founded on rock. And everyone who hears these words of mine and does not act on them will be like a foolish man who built his house on sand. The rain fell, and the floods came, and the winds blew and beat against that house, and it fell—and great was its fall!" (Matthew 7:24-27).

If you've ever watched a house being built, you know that it seems to take a considerable amount of time to prepare the ground and set the foundation. Once that is accomplished, the rest of the building seems to rise relatively quickly. When it is completed, however, the work doesn't end. The home still requires regular maintenance and occasional repairs if it is to withstand the rains, floods, and winds of life.

So it is with our souls, and two things are essential. First, the strength of the foundation determines the stability of the entire structure. It must be set solidly on rock, not shifting sand. Secondly, the inner life of the structure must be filled with the grace of faith in Jesus of which St. Paul speaks: "A person is justified by faith apart from works" (Romans 3:28; cf. Galatians 2:16). One is not opposed to the other. Interior faith must animate our exterior works, and in turn, our works must build our faith (cf. James 2:14-18).

Let us take these words of Christ to heart, so that we remain set solidly on rock without fear of collapsing amid the storms of life, building the Kingdom of Heaven through faith. ♣

# Feasting on the Word

The Word of God is not something outside us. Rather, the Word is a *Person* already written on our hearts. We have only to open ourselves to the presence of the Eternal Word, to *hunger* for the Word made flesh, and then share this Life of Christ with the world.

This is borne out from the first pages of Scripture: God "breathed into [man's] nostrils the breath of life." And as we know from the Gospel of John, "In the beginning was the Word, and the Word was with God, and the Word was God" (1:1). This Word is our very breath!

The power this Word holds for us is demonstrated by Jesus in Matthew 4:1-11. Fasting in the desert for 40 days, Jesus is tempted by Satan three times to turn away from God the Father in ways that should be familiar to us all. Each time, Jesus resists with words from Scripture. "One does not live by bread alone, but by every word that comes from the mouth of God," he declares.

This is inspiration for us all. Jesus was also human. While fasting, he was *hungry*—and not just physically. But when tempted to distrust and disobey God, he turned to the very Word that gives us life because he *is* Life (John 6:27).

As we make our own journey through the wilderness of life, where temptation can serve to strengthen our holy resolve (especially during Lent), let us meditate more deeply on God's gift to us in Word and Sacrament. As Pope Emeritus Benedict XVI said during his General Audience on Ash Wednesday in 2011, "He does not really fast who does not know how to nourish himself on the Word of God. Lent invites us to more faithful and intense prayer and to a prolonged meditation on the Word of God."

These are words not just for Lent, but for life.

# Whom Will You Serve?

We hear a lot today about separation of Church and state. There is considerable tension between the two—and at times, either corrupt collusion or catastrophic conflict. At its core, however, the issue is nothing new. Only the circumstances have changed throughout human history.

In a very real sense, such a tug of war is our own doing. We have created the conditions against which we strain. The real question may be: "What does this perpetual struggle tell us about ourselves, about what we value, about what we desire and strive for?"

From a biblical perspective, the sacred writers relate the answer to us quite clearly:

> What does the Lord your God require of you? Only to fear the Lord your God, to walk in all his ways, to love him, to serve the Lord your God with all your heart and with all your soul, and to keep the commandments of the Lord your God and his decrees that I am commanding you today, for your own well-being. . . . Keep these words that I am commanding you today in your heart. Do not forget the Lord, who brought you out of the land of Egypt, out of the house of slavery. The Lord your God you shall fear; him you shall serve, and by his name alone you shall swear.

> —Deuteronomy 10:12-13; 6:6, 12-13

Later, Joshua tells the chosen People of God: "Choose this day whom you will serve." And the people respond by saying they will serve the Lord, "for it is the Lord our God who brought us and our ancestors up from the land of Egypt, out of the house of slavery, and who did those great signs in our sight. He protected us along all the way that we went, and among all the peoples through whom we passed" (Joshua 24:15, 17).

From the very beginning, humanity was not meant to be governed by anyone but God. The Lord God was King. But our ancestors in the faith, like us, had short memories. It wasn't long before they envied what pagan nations had and chose against God. They pleaded with the prophet and judge Samuel to give them a "real" king: "We are determined to have a king over us, so that we also may be like other nations, and that our king may govern us and go out before us and fight our battles" (1 Samuel 8:19-20).

Samuel resisted, but God told him, "They have not rejected you, but they have rejected me from being king over them." Give them a king, he told Samuel, but warn them what that will mean (1 Samuel 8:6-9). So, Samuel told the people that if he anointed a king over them, their rulers would become greedy, cruel tyrants and thieves, seeking to conquer only for their own personal survival and comfort. Still, they insisted: "Give us a king!"

"Crucify him!" would be the cry many years later, essentially saying the same thing: "We want a king after our *own* image—to rule ourselves. We don't want God."

So, Samuel gave the ancient Israelites a king—Saul—and nations and peoples have been torn asunder ever since (the occasional God-fearing leader notwithstanding; even good leaders make mistakes). This scenario has played out repeatedly over the course of human history. Remarkably, God is still waiting patiently for us to choose the right path.

So what does Jesus mean in Matthew's Gospel (22:15-21) when he says, "Give to the emperor [or Caesar] the things that are the emperor's, and to God the things that are God's"?

First of all, the passage must be considered in context. In the preceding passages in Matthew's Gospel, Jesus has entered Jerusalem, where he knows he will be put to death. He has claimed authority over the temple, and then challenged the religious leaders of the day with parable after parable about unworthy servants. They are offended and angry, and they mean to pay Jesus back everything he has coming to him.

So, the question that the Pharisees and Herodians ask in this Gospel passage—"Is it lawful to pay taxes to the emperor [Caesar], or not?"—is not asked in good faith. The questioners are not interested in the answer, but only in finding a way to do away with Jesus, to put him to death, and get him out of the picture. Their malicious intent is evident in the fact that the Pharisees and Herodians had directly opposing political views (the Pharisees resisted Roman rule, while the Herodians favored it). But they were willing to join forces to get rid of Jesus, and the question they asked was meant to entrap him. There was no right answer.

But Jesus saw through all this, and therefore refused to engage the evil present in the question. Instead, he asked for a coin and asked a question of his own: "Whose head is this, and whose title?"

"The emperor's."

"Give therefore to the emperor the things that are the emperor's, and to God the things that are God's." (Here, I can envision him flipping the coin back to the group.)

With this answer, Jesus is not taking any position on the issue of separation of Church and state. He is not advocating any human government or revolutionary movement. Instead, he implies that the very conditions giving rise to the question are a result of our own sinfulness, our turning away from the God who made us. He may as well have said, "*You* asked for a king!"

And that is the key to the whole episode. The religious leaders still want a human ruler, a king, even though the King of kings, God of gods, stands directly in front of them. Like Joshua, Jesus again is asking the question, "Choose this day whom you will serve."

So, whatever choice is placed in front of us, we must ask ourselves in Jesus' own words: "Whose head is this, and whose title?" If the answer is, "the emperor's," then we must act accordingly. However, what it all boils down to is this: Each one of us—even "the emperor"—is *made in the image of God*. God's image is imprinted on every human heart, just as Caesar's image was imprinted on ancient Roman coins. Whether we acknowledge it or not, it is God to whom we belong and whom we must love and serve—with all our heart, soul, and mind. Give to "the emperor" the things that are the emperor's, and to God the things that are God's.

As Jesus says elsewhere: "Where your treasure is, there your heart will be also" (Matthew 6:21). ♣

# The Word at Work

Scripture in many places offers sound advice for all who are entrusted with positions of leadership. And really, that includes each and every one of us. In one way or another, each of us has someone in his or her charge—whether it's children, siblings, employees, patients, constituents, parishioners, etc. Even friends and co-workers. *Someone* is looking to each of us to set the example in some regard.

While each of us fails in varying degrees to set a good example 100 percent of the time, the ideal leader in each one of us must strive to serve our brothers and sisters and recognize that we all have one Father in heaven.

Several passages in the Bible tell us how *not* to do this, how we so often fail (e.g. Malachi 1:14b-2:2b, 8-10 and Matthew 23:1-12). But sprinkled liberally throughout many Scripture texts are ideas worth taking to heart in a positive sense. For example, St. Paul (in 1 Thessalonians 2:7b-9, 13) outlines the right attitude for us all. As leaders in our daily lives, we must be:

*Gentle*

*Caring*

*Affectionate*

*Self-sacrificing*

*Hard-working*

*Willing to bear another's burdens.*

*Willing to proclaim God's Word in word and deed.*

*Grateful*

*Generous*

In short, Christians of any state or position in life are to serve one another and the world under one Father in heaven, just as Jesus did. "For the Son of Man came not to be served but to serve, and to give his life as a ransom for many" (Mark 10:45). This call is the same of us all, though it is carried out in various ways. No matter our rank, we all have but one master, the Christ, "who, though he was in the form of God, did not regard equality with God as something to be exploited, but emptied himself, taking the form of a slave . . . Therefore God also highly exalted him" (Philippians 2:6-7, 9).

This is the Word of God now at work in you who believe. ♣

# A Wise Investment

As Christian people, we must be properly disposed and prepare ourselves for the second coming of Christ. We both wait and work for the Kingdom of God. Through the Holy Spirit, and with the aid of Scripture, the sacraments, the tradition of the Church and all those within it, God is among us. "The Kingdom of God is among you," Jesus tells us (Luke 17:21).

This is a particularly important point to consider annually when we approach the beginning of Advent and the Christmas season, when we commemorate the first coming of Christ. But it does not—*should* not—end there. In Matthew's Gospel (25:14-30), Jesus tells his disciples a parable about a man going on a journey (clearly referring to himself after his Death, Resurrection, and Ascension) who entrusts his wealth to his servants (referring to his disciples, both at that time and in these days). This is remarkable. Through no merit of their own, these servants are entrusted with their master's possessions. He gives it to them freely to do as they please until he returns.

Each of them receives a different amount—according to his ability, as the text says—but in every case it is no small portion, even for the third servant receiving the least. Just *one* talent in the time of Jesus was a HUGE amount of money. An absurd amount, actually. Today, it would be like an extremely wealthy individual giving one person $5 billion, another $2 billion, and the third $1 billion. So, the last, while receiving less, still receives an incredible amount of money.

However, this parable is not about money, nor is it referring merely to the special individual talents and material possessions we have. Also at stake, and even more important, are the many spiritual gifts bestowed upon us—each according to his or her ability. Some are given great humility; others are granted great spiritual wisdom or knowledge, while still others may display remarkable fortitude or charity in serving others.

The list is endless. By the grace of God, even the "poorest" among us is incredibly rich in some way. As the beginning of the Gospel of John says, from the fullness of Christ we all receive "grace upon grace" (1:16).

Why all these different gifts? Why do some seem to receive more of one and less of another? Why do we not *each* receive *everything* we could possibly need—the five talents, or $5 billion, as it were?

The answer is a wonderful mystery to contemplate: the distribution is unequal so that we each receive what we need from others. *God wills us to need one another!* No one sins or is saved by his or her self. We must each share in some way the grace we have been given. We must invest it in one another to bear fruit for the building of the Kingdom of God, just as the servant with five talents did, and the one with two. Each took what he had been freely given and traded with others to grow even richer—making others richer in the process (cf. *Catechism of the Catholic Church*, 1936-1937). As the Lord told St. Catherine of Siena in a vision, "I have willed that one should need another and that all should be my ministers in distributing the graces and gifts they have received from me."

Those who do so "enter into the joy" of the master—now, and most fully, in the Eternal Kingdom. Grace must be invested, not conserved. We not only wait for the Kingdom of God, but as the Body of Christ *participate now* in its building. The Christian life is one of participation in the gifts of the Holy Spirit that Christ has breathed into us through Scripture, the sacraments, the tradition of the Church and all those within it. We are called to enter into our master's joy by making one another rich in the things of God. As Jesus says in the Gospel of John, "The one who believes in me will also do the works that I do and, in fact, will do greater works than these, because I am going to the Father" (John 14:12).

Stop and re-read that last sentence again. We are called to do GREATER works than Jesus accomplished during his time on earth!!! That is amazing!

But we don't do them alone. We do them through the grace entrusted to us by Christ and shared with one another. "I am the vine, you are the branches," Jesus says. "Those who abide in me and I in them bear much fruit, because apart from me you can do nothing" (John 15:5).

God is absurdly lavish with us. He entrusts the wealth of his Kingdom to us. He allows us to work with him in building it up. The first two servants in Matthew's parable, though receiving different amounts, participate equally in the building of the Kingdom because they invested what had been gratuitously given to them.

The third servant, however, did not merely neglect to do this. He *refused* to help, to invest the enormous talent entrusted to him. Even worse, when it came time to settle accounts upon the master's return, he blames it all on the master, contemptuously claiming that he had been paralyzed by fear, and offering back only what he had been given. The punishment was not unjust. He had chosen it; he had refused to enter into his master's joy, deciding to selfishly hold on to what had been given him rather than allowing others to benefit—as the others had done with their investment in the Kingdom.

The third servant hoped for the future Kingdom without *participating* in its present manifestation. How could he then share in what he had not helped to build?

We must ask ourselves the same question. The most successful corporations, sports teams, and other organizations in our secular world know that building a rich future means investing in the present. It's the only wise investment to make in sacred matters as well. The third servant bet on the future by forfeiting the present, and lost it all as a result.

In his generosity, God has entrusted the Kingdom to us. The grace we have been given is not ours to keep, but to share so that it may bear fruit for others. So, we must ask ourselves each day: How am I investing the spiritual wealth entrusted to me for the future of the Body of Christ? How am I being faithful in small matters so that I may enter into God's tremendous joy? Who today needs the grace which has been granted to me, and whose grace may I likewise benefit from? ♠

# Faith in the Familiar

**F**amiliarity breeds contempt, the saying goes. We think we know a person, have him or her figured out, and are familiar with his or her background, thought processes, attributes. Nothing, we think, that he or she can do, or say, will surprise us.

Impossible! No person thoroughly knows another, no matter how close they are, how much time they spend with one another, or how long they have known one another. Even the most intimate of companions or spouses have unexamined or developing aspects of themselves. One's skin contains only one person, and even he or she doesn't fully comprehend who that person is or will become. Only the Creator of all knows all, as recounted in Psalm 139:

> *O Lord, it was you who formed my inward parts;*
> *    you knit me together in my mother's womb.*
> *. . . Your eyes beheld my unformed substance.*
> *In your book were written all the days*
> *    that were formed for me,*
> *    when none of them as yet existed.*

When we human beings think we really know someone (*thinking we are God?*), we tend to miss or dismiss their potential, to impose superficial limits on our own perspective (and that of others)—and, quite possibly, on the capabilities of the person in question. We observe someone and then shake our heads, cluck our tongues, and say, "He's always been that way."

Another opportunity lost!

I once worked with someone who, at the beginning of the shift, would smile, rub his hands, and proclaim, "I'm excited about the possibilities!" It was an inside joke in a difficult work environment, but he also really meant it. His was a voice of optimism in what could be an otherwise negative atmosphere. His proclamation gave me hope—and no small measure of amusement.

Such an attitude opens doors, presents fresh opportunities, and brings to light new perspectives. At its core, this is *faith*, pure and simple.

Applying this to our relationship with a person we may *think* we know all too well, we should ask ourselves: *Can I allow myself to be excited about the possibilities; to be open to a new encounter with the same old, same old; to see and hear the presence of Christ within another person despite (or because of) all that I think I know about that person?*

In the gospels, Jesus tells us that we are to find him in one another (cf. Matthew 25:31-46). So, in this light, we also should ask ourselves: *Am I able to have faith in Christ's presence in the* familiar, *in what and whom I know (or think I know)?*

Even Jesus was taken for granted by those who knew him, as illustrated in Mark's Gospel (6:1-6). Familiarity—even with Jesus—bred contempt. Jesus attempts to proclaim the Good News in his native place, but is met with scorn by those who have known him for quite some time: "Where did this man get all this? . . . Is this not the carpenter, the son of Mary. . .?" In other words: "Who does he *think* he is? *We* know him, where he came from. He's got some nerve trying to tell us what's what!"

And so Jesus laments, "Prophets are not without honor, except in their hometown, and among their own kin, and in their own house."

Those who were (arguably) most familiar with Jesus exhibited a remarkable lack of faith. Because of this, we are told that Jesus "could do no deed of power there . . . He was amazed at their unbelief."

Familiarity is often an obstacle to faith—for all of us. And without faith, we will not experience God's presence and mighty works. We do well to regularly ask ourselves: *Do I too easily dismiss the familiar (whether it's a person, thing, or circumstance? Or do I look in faith for the possibilities?*

As flawed human beings, we tend to place a disproportionate amount of belief in strength, outward beauty, and wealth. When someone seemingly *without* such qualities—even Jesus—presents us with a prophetic challenge to look with an open heart at what and whom is all too familiar, it is easy to overlook, dismiss, or scorn. We often forget that "power is made perfect in weakness" (2 Corinthians 12:9), and that such power is the only remedy for the original sin of human pride. In this way—embracing weakness—God became man, was born of a virgin, was quietly raised in humble circumstances, performed mighty deeds and taught great truths within the ordinariness of human living, was betrayed and crucified as a common criminal . . . and then was resurrected.

Jesus' words call each of us to look with the eyes of faith at everything and everyone around us, to see the presence of Christ, to detect brand-new possibilities within the familiar, and to acknowledge the power inherent in the "weakness" of another. *What can this familiar person, this thing, this circumstance, teach me today?* We are called to hear the prophetic witness of the Good News from the most unlikely of sources, and to acknowledge that as much as we know, we *really* don't know. . . Except, that is, through faith in the Person of Christ, who is all in all (cf. Ephesians 1:23). When we allow him to enter our hearts, we can then ask, as did the inhabitants of Jerusalem on Palm Sunday: "Who is this?" (Matthew 21:10). Then, the knowledge of who Jesus is will truly reveal who we are in relation to God and one another.

Through faith, the power of God's Word—Jesus Christ—is made perfect in what is familiar and weak. 🌰

# God's Calling Plan

Just who were the Twelve Apostles, really? Nobody special. They were not high-class, or well-educated, or upstanding citizens. Quite the contrary is true. They did not apply for the position, and they were not vetted for particular credentials. In fact, they were not qualified at all.

And yet, unqualified, unprepared and flawed as they were, Jesus "called" them, as Mark's Gospel states (6:7-13). He sent them out to preach the gospel, gave them authority, and instructed them. *He* chose *them*, and then *he* qualified them. "You did not choose me but I chose you," Jesus says in the Gospel of John (15:16); "Apart from me, you can do nothing" (15:5).

The prophet Amos, prefiguring the Christian response to God's call long before Jesus' time, knew the nature of this gift. "I am no prophet, nor a prophet's son," he says. "I am a herdsman, and a dresser of sycamore trees, and the Lord took me from following the flock, and the Lord said to me, 'Go, prophesy to my people.'" And so he went—nobody special, yet accomplishing God's work (Amos 7:12-15).

Today, all Christians have precisely the same call—in different ways and circumstances, to be sure, but the call to live and preach the gospel is universal. Not everyone hears the call, or responds to it. Some take their time answering. Others simply (and sadly) refuse. But the call is there.

In a beautiful and theologically rich passage from the Letter to the Ephesians (1:3-14), we are told that God blesses and chooses each one of us "before the foundation of the world." Think about that for a minute. It's an astounding declaration. Before the One God in Three Persons created the universe, before anyone was born, before Jesus as God the Son came into the world, *God chose us.* Otherwise, we simply would not *be.* And knowing us completely—more fully than we will ever know ourselves—God understood beforehand how unqualified we would be, how unprepared, how flawed. He knew that we would all turn away from him, would sin, and would know failure, sorrow, and pain.

Yet he *still* chose us. He knew before anything *was* that Jesus would enter into a point in time to show us the way to God. He knew that a Savior would be necessary before sin existed, before *we* existed—to make us holy, to adopt us, to redeem us, to make himself known to us, and to involve us in his plan to "gather up all things" in Christ (Ephesians 1:10). As St. Paul says elsewhere, "God proves his love for us in that while we still were sinners Christ died for us" (Romans 5:8). We are, as the Letter to the Ephesians says, chosen and destined by a God who accomplishes all things, to "live for the praise of his glory."

This is a wonderful mystery that cannot be fully grasped. We must simply let it grasp us, guide us. But that is difficult to do, isn't it?

A couple years before coming to the monastery, I had a discussion with a very wise priest. I knew I was being called to something new, to something that was both exciting and terrifying, simply because it was unknown. I felt totally overwhelmed and unqualified for whatever it was that God had in store for me (at that time I didn't know precisely what it was, but I felt the pull, so to speak). "I can't do it," I told the priest. He listened to my reasons, and then gently said, "If God is calling you to something, he will give you everything you need to accomplish it. Do not be afraid. He is always with you."

It took me a while longer to realize that indeed, God calls first; *then* he qualifies. We do not—and cannot—qualify ourselves first. Once I was granted the grace to understand that, I was able to make a leap of faith that I never could have foreseen; such an act went completely against the grain of how I typically operated. In fact, some people thought I had gone nuts!

New parents, no doubt, feel completely overwhelmed and unqualified. But God calls each newborn child into this world and into the lives of his/her parents for a reason. With the infant's unwitting (and malodorous) assistance, God qualifies each parent *after* choosing them. Years later, each child is called along his or her own vocational path. In one way or another, each of us is called to participate in God's plan to "gather up all things" in Christ.

At one level, these Scripture passages revolve around vocation, and the fact that everybody has one where God is concerned. No one is qualified. No one is prepared. Everyone is flawed. Yet God still calls. However, at a still deeper level, Scripture emphasizes God's initiative and his providence. We love because he first loved us before the foundation of the world (cf. 1 John 4:19; John 1:1-5).

Ultimately, vocation is not about what we *do*, but about who we *are*. Just like the Apostles, we are nobody special—but chosen nonetheless. We are chosen by God to give what we do not have, to bestow in Christ every spiritual blessing from absolute nothingness, to live in the mystery of God's will in order to gather up all things in Christ. And he is with us each step of the way. ♠

# Choosing the Wise Path

J ust as Jesus is tempted by the devil in the wilderness (cf. Luke 4:1-13), each of one of us is tempted on a daily basis to choose the ways of the world over the ways of God. What are the ways of the world? Primarily, "worldly wisdom" teaches that health and wealth, success, and influence (or power) are the ultimate values in life. We want to be disease- and injury-free, prosperous, triumphant, and in control of not only our own destinies, but often those of other people and events as well.

It is neither wrong nor evil to have or experience such things. What really matters is to what extent these gifts are valued by us, how they're obtained, and how they are put to use. Each of these things, depending on our interior motivations and attachments, can be either the means of honoring God or foolishly forsaking him by making them idols.

The truly wise one, according to our Christian faith, is the one who recognizes that "the fear of the Lord is the beginning of wisdom" (Proverbs 9:10). This is not a cowering, servile fear. It is grateful recognition of God as the Giver of all good gifts, and ourselves as his stewards and ambassadors responding in love to his divine goodness.

Choosing the wisdom of God also is not a once-in-a-lifetime event, but an ongoing struggle to discern and act rightly. As Scripture scholar and author Barbara Bowe pointed out in her book *Biblical Foundations of Spirituality,* "In the daily rhythms of life each one must choose between the ways of the wise and the ways of the foolish. In choosing the wise path, we choose the path of life."

These choices are laid out in front of us every day in myriad ways. Each day, we must make constant choices as to whether to serve oneself or serve others out of love for Christ. Strengthened by that love, let us answer the temptation to act according to the world's ways with the same words Jesus spoke to combat the devil in the wilderness: "Worship the Lord your God, and serve only him."

# Faith

# Building Blocks

"Lord, we do not know where you are going. How can we know the way?" the Apostle Thomas asks Jesus (John 14:5). It is a prayer most of us have prayed at one time or another: "Lord, I don't understand. What is going on? Why is this happening? Where is it taking me? What do you have in store for me? How can I know your will, your purpose in this? Help me to know."

Jesus' response is one of reassurance. In the previous chapter of John's Gospel, he encourages his disciples through word and deed to love and serve one another in the face of betrayal, suffering, and persecution. He was speaking of his own impending death, but was also foretelling the trials his disciples would face—then and now. The Eternal Word of Christ resounds throughout history, and what he says is just as true for us as it was for his first disciples. "Do not let your hearts be troubled," he says. "Believe in God, believe also in me. I am the way, and the truth, and the life" (John 14:1, 6).

In other words: "Have faith!"

There is a point where we simply have to let go and let God, as the popular saying goes. We are living stones, as the Letter of St. Peter says, in God's spiritual house (1 Peter 2:5). God builds us up, and Christ is the cornerstone on which we are fastened. The trouble is that we often wish to do the building according to our *own* designs when God has other—much better—plans.

In faith, as God's living stones, we must do what St. Peter urges: "*Let* yourselves be built into a spiritual house." Not build, but *be* built. There is a difference.

We are the work of God, and in him we dwell.

# Believing, Belonging, Building

L ove is not a feeling. It certainly *involves* feelings, but ultimately it must go much, much deeper. More than anything else, love is a *decision*. True love is not always pleasant or easy, but it is *always* fulfilling because in demanding total giving of self, it paradoxically delivers genuine self-realization. It is other-directed, but self-discovering, in that order. Love is a manifestation of the self-giving of the God of Love, who exhaled his own divine breath of life into us, and later, in the person of Jesus, exhaled his last human breath to give us eternal life despite all our wrongdoing and ingratitude.

Faith is similar. It is not a feeling, though at times it may involve feelings. Ultimately, it is a *commitment*. It doesn't mean seeing or knowing everything, but believing in the One who does—the God who leads us just as he led the ancient Israelites out of slavery and across the desert to the Promised Land. Faith, like love, is a relationship of trust that seeks the good, even when it is not self-evident. Faith is, as the celebrated declaration in the Letter to the Hebrews says, "the assurance of things hoped for, the conviction of things not seen" (11:1).

Culminating with the Incarnation, God gradually manifested himself on Earth (the manna in the desert, Jesus' feeding of 5,000 people with a few barley loves, the Eucharist, etc.). He became one with our human nature, but sometimes (likely *most* times) all we can see is the earthly reality. That's OK. Faith asks us nevertheless to trust in the divine presence of self-giving in our relationship with God and with one another—to believe in what is said because of *who* has said it: "I am the Bread of Life" (John 6:35); "This is my Son, the Beloved; listen to him!" (Mark 9:7).

Faith is a free choice to profess one's belonging to One greater than one's own self, to regularly renew our individual and collective commitment of belonging to God. The ancient Israelites, under the leadership of Joshua, did this upon entering the Promised Land, and we do this at every Eucharist under the leadership of Jesus (Joshua and Jesus are different forms of the same name in Hebrew).

As Christians, we do well to meditate on what the commitment of belonging truly means in terms of our relationship with God and with one another. *How has God manifested himself to me? What does it mean for me today?* Several passages in Scripture offer worthy points of reflection in this regard. Among them:

*"Choose this day whom you will serve"* (Joshua 24:15).

*"Be subject to one another out of reverence for Christ"* (Ephesians 5:21).

*"Do you also wish to go away?"* (John 6:67).

Peter gives the perfect response in John's Gospel: "Lord, to whom can we go? You have the words of eternal life. We have come to believe and know that you are the Holy One of God" (6:60-69).

As we know, Peter, first and foremost among the Apostles and the rock upon which the Church is built, did not always live that response perfectly—even *after* this conversation in John's Gospel. That should give us *all* hope. By the grace and mercy of God, to paraphrase St. Anthony the Great, each day we begin again, deciding whom we will serve.

Let us each day choose to taste and see that the Lord is good, and commit to building up one another in the love of Christ. ⚜

# We Know Not How It Grows

A s beautiful as it is, nature can sometimes seem harsh and indiscriminate—whether it's the environment we're talking about, humanity itself, or all the natural forces that direct them. The storms of life fell many trees in the world, both literally and figuratively, and the body, mind, and soul are not exempted.

While it is necessary and healthy to survey and mourn the damage wrought by the occasional tempest, focusing on it can severely limit or distort our perception of all the good surrounding the storm—or even arising *from* it. We must, as St. Paul says, "walk by faith, not by sight" (2 Corinthians 5:7).

Life certainly takes many unexpected twists and turns, but God's promise to us is that he is *always* at work in the world—whether we see it or not, or even whether we believe it or not. Like a tiny seed slowly sprouting, taking root, maturing, blooming, and striving toward the sun, the Kingdom of God continues to grow upward and outward. "See, I am making all things new," God promises, for "all things work together for good for those who love God" (cf. Revelation 21:5; Romans 8:28).

As Jesus states in Mark's Gospel (4:26-34), "The kingdom of God is as if someone would scatter seed on the ground, and would sleep and rise night and day, and the seed would sprout and grow, he does not know how." God gently beckons every withered tree to bloom, put forth branches, and bear fruit, so that all may dwell beneath the shade of the Almighty (cf. Ezekiel 17:23-25; Mark 4:32).

By God's promise and grace, through the Tree of Life that is Christ, the Kingdom of God is sprouting and growing night and day, in war and peace, in raging storms and restful stillness . . . though we know not how.

# Healing Faith

"Show me where it hurts," a concerned parent or physician may say to an ill or injured child, who then moves his or her hand to the trouble spot. With that knowledge, the parent or physician touches and examines the area to assess the problem and apply a remedy.

There are numerous references in the gospels to physical touch and healing. For example: "Come and lay your hands on" my daughter, Jairus pleads with Jesus. Meanwhile, the crowd "pressed in on" Jesus. An ill but hopeful woman "touched his cloak." Jesus takes Jairus' dead daughter "by the hand" and restores her to life (Mark 5:21-43).

Given the social circumstances and religious customs of the time, all this touching of, and by Jesus, has enormous spiritual implications. By touching Jesus, the hemorrhaging woman rendered him ritually unclean and unable to worship in the temple. By touching the dead body of the 12-year-old girl, Jesus rendered himself ritually unclean. Yet both are cured. The power of God overcomes illness and death, the common human condition that is the result of humanity's turning away from God.

God breaks through *all* barriers to restore humanity to its rightful relationship with him and one another. So, we are compelled to press upon him, touch him, and be cured.

*But where is he? How do I find him? How can I touch him?*

You can't. Instead, *he touches us.* God became man, placed himself amid the pressing crowd of humanity, and took on our indignity to restore our dignity. As with Jairus' daughter, Christ takes each of us by the hand and says, "Get up!" How? In prayer, in the Eucharist, in Confession and all the Sacraments, in the Word of God, in the life and tradition of the Church, in the love of Christ that we share with one another through the Holy Spirit. Through these means, God touches us, heals us, and calls us to new life.

Yes, the world and the Church are filled with problems, with scandals, with sins. For now, the wheat and the weeds grow together (cf. Matthew 13:25-30). But God is in our midst, asking us where it hurts, touching us, offering us hope and healing. It's there for the taking. It's free. All the rest will eventually fall away.

In the meantime, only one thing is required, and Jesus explicitly spells it out in the passage from Mark's Gospel. What does he say to both the hemorrhaging woman and Jairus?

"Your *faith* has made you well."

"Do not fear, only *believe*."

While we can pray and hope for physical cures, for earthly miracles, Jesus is offering us something much greater—*someone* much greater: himself. It is through his touch—in Word, sacrament, prayer, the life of the Church, in charity—that the Second Person of the Holy Trinity leads us to eternal life, to a share in his divinity. This occurs through the faith that God alone can give the heart that is willing to receive it.

In his weekly *Angelus* address on July 1, 2012, Pope Emeritus Benedict XVI stated all this much better than I ever could. He says:

> These two stories of healing are an invitation for us to overcome a purely horizontal and materialistic view of life. So often we ask God to cure our problems, to relieve our concrete needs—and this is right. But what we should ask for even more is an ever stronger *faith*, because the Lord renews our lives; and a firm trust in his love, in his providence that does not abandon us.

"Show me where it hurts," God tells his children.

The Divine Physician takes us by the hand and says, "Be healed of your disease."

God touches us, and like a parent soothing a frightened child, whispers softly:

"Do not fear, only believe." ♠

# Think BIG

It must have been awfully surprising and also disappointing for all those people crowded into the house in Capernaum who had come to listen to Jesus speak in Mark's Gospel (2:1-12). They had heard about the miracles, the healings Jesus had performed, and were eager to experience one in person. Then, when the roof was opened above them, and a paralytic was lowered down on a mat in front of Jesus, everyone must have held their breath with anticipation. "Here it comes—watch this!" many may have whispered.

Then Jesus looks at the paralytic and says, "Son, your sins are forgiven."

*What? That's it? Where's the cure? We were expecting a miracle! What a disappointment! We walked all the way over here for this? No one but God can forgive sins, anyway. This guy's a fraud!*

Even the learned scribes present couldn't see the true miracle that had occurred right in front of them. They began to scoff and condemn Jesus.

But the paralytic knew what had happened. What peace he must have experienced deep throughout his soul as he looked back at Jesus while everyone around them was caught up in their own expectations and judgments. *His sins were forgiven, wiped away, removed forever!*

Of course, such a miracle—a *true* miracle—could not be seen outwardly, but only with the eyes of faith. The forgiveness of sins by God is the "new thing" foretold by Isaiah (43:18-19, 21-22, 24b-25). "I am he who blots out your transgressions for my own sake, and I will not remember your sins," God says. "Your sins are forgiven."

This is what we as human beings truly need (and truly want, at least unconsciously), but like the crowd in Mark's Gospel, we sell God short. We think small, while God thinks BIG. We want physical healings, miracles, things we can see with our eyes and be amazed by. Trapped within our own expectations, we doubt anything we can't see. Anything we do see, we instantly judge according to those preconceived notions. Too often, we remain focused solely on the external.

This must have grieved Jesus in the Gospel story. *He had saved a soul.* However, everyone but the paralytic (and possibly his friends) expected less than what God wanted to give. They expected Jesus to heal this man's body.

*"What? That's easy!"* Jesus said, in so many words. *"Can't you see what I have done, what the forgiveness of sins means for this man and for all of you?"* He must have sighed at the crowd's lack of faith that was so evident to him in the paralytic's friends. "But so that you may know that the Son of Man has authority on earth to forgive sins, [then, turning to the forgiven paralytic] I say to you, stand up, take your mat and go to your home" (Mark 2:10-11).

He did. And only *then* was the crowd astounded.

God wants to give us so much more than we expect. He did not become man to remove our physical suffering. He certainly came to console us in our trials, to *share* in our suffering, and to take upon himself all our burdens, even to death on a cross. But he did this primarily to forgive our sins, to heal our souls which were broken by the Fall of humanity. He came to restore to us what we had lost—eternal union with God the Father, the Son, and the Holy Spirit.

And to do this, he inserted himself into a time and culture that directly associated sin with physical and mental illness and disability. He performed external healing to signify internal healing, to show us that God saves souls from sin, that he means what he says and that we should settle for nothing less.

The Hebrew form of Jesus, after all, means *God saves.* "I am about to do a new thing; now it springs forth, do you not perceive it?" God says (Isaiah 43:19). *Think BIG!*

St. Paul states, "It is God who establishes us with you in Christ and has anointed us, by putting his seal on us and giving us his Spirit in our hearts as a first installment" (2 Corinthians 1:21-22). God is faithful, and when we lower ourselves before him in faith, no matter how imperfect or paralyzed by sin we may be, he says to us, "Your sins are forgiven. Stand up, take your mat and go to your home." ♣

# Ponder This

*The shepherds went with haste and found Mary and Joseph,*
*and the child lying in the manger. When they saw this,*
*they made known what had been told them about this child;*
*and all who heard it were amazed at what the shepherds told them.*
*But Mary treasured all these words and pondered them in her heart.*

—Luke 2:16-19

It is interesting that when God becomes man, and the Savior of the world is born to redeem and reconcile humankind, it is a group of shepherds that first tells the world about the Christ. Meanwhile, Mary, the Mother of God, says nothing. Rather, she "treasured all these words and *pondered* them in her heart." Mary was silent as she considered the fruit of creation, the great mystery of God that is too great for words to express.

God's promise of salvation had been revealed in Jesus and was at that very moment growing toward the fulfillment that was later realized in the passion, death, and resurrection of Christ. This growth continues today in Christ's mystical body, the Church that is anointed with the heavenly dew of the Holy Spirit. Silently it grows, though we know not how (cf. Mark 4:27). This is the mystery Mary treasured and pondered in her heart on the night the Eternal Word sprouted from her womb. The same treasure is ours, if we listen as Mary did to the voice of the Lord, which is written in our hearts (cf. Deuteronomy 30:14; Romans 10:8).

Most of Mary's life was hidden and unremarkable. She lived day to day, fulfilling her duties, but with faith in the promise that had been announced to her and Joseph. Although she had said yes to this promise and had placed her hope in it, she did not fully understand. She was left to silently ponder each thing that occurred during her daily life as it slowly unfolded.

The Greek word for ponder means "to piece together." This is what Mary did, storing up all these events in her heart, constantly reflecting on them, wondering about them, trusting in them. It is in our trust that we praise God, not in complete understanding.

Pope Emeritus Benedict XVI spoke of this pondering in a 2008 homily on the Solemnity of Mary, Mother of God:

> By learning from Mary, we can understand with our hearts what our eyes and minds do not manage to perceive or contain on their own. Indeed, this is such a great gift that only through faith are we granted to accept it, while not entirely understanding it. And it is precisely on this journey of faith that Mary comes to meet us as our support and guide. . . . In her heart Mary continued to treasure, to "piece together" [the events of her life with Jesus]. . . . It is only by pondering in the heart, in other words, by piecing together and finding unity in all we experience that, following Mary, we can penetrate the mystery of a God who was made man out of love and who calls us to follow him on that path of love; a love to be expressed daily by generous service [to our brothers and sisters].

Ultimately, this path of love leads to the passion, death, and resurrection of Christ. This is where Mary was able finally to put it all together, and where we also are each called as the Body of Christ. It is not easy. It is sometimes painful, exhausting, and sorrowful. But beyond the horizon of our vision, the awesome Love of God flowers and conquers all—the same Love whom God sent in his Son, born of a woman. With him, in him, and through him, we are God's children.

Let us be still and ponder. Let us treasure God's loving presence. Let us pray that we listen for and remain receptive to the seed of God's Word sown in our own hearts so that it may grow, spread, and bear fruit for the Kingdom of God—though we know not how.

And when our strength fails us, let us always turn to Mary our Mother, who embraces in her arms the Body of Christ—whether as an infant wrapped in swaddling clothes or an adult stripped of all dignity, bruised and beaten on Calvary. With Mary's faithfulness, we are assured of finally grasping the last piece of the puzzle: that what is broken emerges whole and transformed from an empty tomb—in the ponderable silence of the dawn. ♣

# Remember

Christians are called to be a people of gratitude. And to be truly grateful, we must take the time to *remember* all that God has done for us. As St. Paul says: "Remember Jesus Christ, raised from the dead" (2 Timothy 2:8).

In the Second Book of Kings (5:14-17), Naaman the Syrian, after having been cleansed of his leprosy, remembers to give praise to God. In Luke's Gospel (17:11-19), the Samaritan, healed by Jesus along with nine other lepers, is the only one to remember to glorify God. Jesus tells him, "Your faith has made you well."

It is important to recognize that diseases such as leprosy were associated with sin in an ancient world not yet acquainted with our modern medical advances. So these texts, as do so many others in Scripture, point to something beyond miraculous physical cures. They speak of God's desire to heal us spiritually. What's more, they present the theme of universal salvation. Both Naaman and the Samaritan were not only lepers, but foreigners and outsiders. They were not considered a part of God's people. Yet they were healed because God's generosity excludes no one.

As God's people today, do we *remember* that generosity, and express daily through lives of faith our gratitude to the God who heals all? ❧

# Hosanna, Exclamation Point

L ike many events in life, our annual celebration of Palm Sunday of the Lord's Passion seems to offer an odd mixture of jubilant anticipation and terrifying confusion. We begin by recalling Jesus' procession into Jerusalem with his disciples, holding palm branches and proclaiming "*Hosanna!*" We end having proceeded through the events surrounding Jesus' passion, which concludes with the Son of God's lifeless body sealed in a tomb. It is enough to make one's head spin!

However, a certain measure of disorientation is perhaps necessary if we are to genuinely enter into the mysteries of Holy Week, and in turn, incorporate those very mysteries into our ordinary living. Profound clarity and renewed life can arise from momentary disorientation. Sometimes, we *need* to be bewildered in such a way in order to focus more clearly on the Truth underlying daily lives that can seem to rapidly unfold without any direction or purpose.

In times of contradiction and confusion, we are often led inwardly to ask ourselves: "What is *really* important? How am I striving for it? Where do I go from here?" Such examination can help us reorient our lives toward God in new and meaningful ways.

While pondering these questions, two points are worth consideration. First, as Pope Emeritus Benedict XVI points out in his book *Jesus of Nazareth, Part II: Holy Week, The Entrance into Jerusalem to the Resurrection*, the proclamation *Hosanna*, derived from an ancient Hebrew term basically meaning "God, save us!" (cf. Psalm 118:25), is a simultaneous expression of petition, praise, and hope all in one. Its reply, quite simply, is "*Jesus*," which in Hebrew means "God saves."

Secondly, the high point of the Palm Sunday liturgy, just as it is at every Mass, is not the moment when we recall Jesus' death, but the consecration and reception of his body and blood in the Eucharist: "This is my body, which will be given up for you." What Jesus offers us in himself is LIFE, as recalled from his exclamation in John's Gospel: "I am the resurrection and the life" (11:25). God saves and gives us life through the death and resurrection of Christ.

Regarding this integral association of the Resurrection with the Eucharist, Benedict writes, "The Day of Resurrection is the exterior and interior locus of Christian worship, and the thanksgiving prayer [at the Last Supper] as Jesus' creative anticipation of the Resurrection is the Lord's way of uniting us with his thanksgiving, blessing us in the gift, and drawing us into the process of transformation that starts with the gifts, moves on to include us, and then spreads out to the world until he comes."

You may also recall God's promise to the prophet Ezekiel: "I am going to open your graves, and bring you up from your graves!" (37:12). And so, on Palm Sunday (at least during those years when the Passion from the Gospel of Matthew is read or sung), we hear that at the same disorienting moment of Jesus' death, "the earth shook, and the rocks were split. The tombs also were opened, and many *bodies of the saints who had fallen asleep were raised*" (Matthew 27:51-52).

Once again, profound clarity and renewed life can arise from momentary disorientation. Apparent defeat gives way to true victory.

That message's exclamation point—which we celebrate each Easter Sunday and on every Sunday throughout the year—is an everyday reality.

So, what *is* really important? *How* am I striving for it? *Where* do I go from here? ♠

*Hope*

# Light Shines in the Darkness

Darkness blankets the earth. Night descends and we seek rest, security, and peace. The dawn promises hope, newness, and joy, but it is a long time coming. Sleep is elusive, fear and worry creep in, and loneliness torments. We toss and turn throughout the long night.

Under the cover of night, we are haunted by the demons of war, oppression, violence, injustice, poverty, racism, disparity, corruption, crime, abuse, lust, greed, selfishness, jealousy, anger, conflict, hostility, isolation, guilt, shame, despair, depression, exhaustion, addiction, illness, pain, grief, sorrow, and death. All the result of the sin of pride inherited from our first parents, humanity's choice to spurn the God of all and "be like God" ourselves (cf. Genesis 3:5).

It is a dark, dark world—like Pottersville in Frank Capra's 1946 film "It's a Wonderful Life." Except that Pottersville didn't exist. It *would* have existed if it had not been for one man, George Bailey, famously portrayed by Jimmy Stewart. His goodness, his light, kept the evil darkness of Mr. Potter at bay. His light provided hope for the good people of Bedford Falls. And when the darkness threatened to overtake even poor, desperate George Bailey, something small and wonderful happened:

*God stepped in.*

So it is with us. While "It's a Wonderful Life" provides an apt metaphor for God's presence in the world, the Incarnation we recall in the feast of Christmas each year surpasses all wonder. God became man. God entered the darkness—not to eradicate humanity's woes, but to give them meaning and purpose within a fallen world grasping at straws. Christ is our hope in a world of darkness. His "light shines in the darkness, and the darkness did not overcome it" (John 1:5).

The theme of light piercing the darkness is prevalent throughout Scripture and in the Church's liturgy, especially at Christmas. "The people who walked in darkness have seen a great light; those who lived in a land of deep darkness—on them light has shined," prophesies Isaiah (9:1-6). "The grace of God has appeared," writes St. Paul (Titus 2:11-14). "The glory of the Lord shone around" the shepherds as the angel of the Lord announced the birth of Jesus (Luke 2:1-14).

It is interesting to note that this light of God's glory *does not eliminate* the dark night. Rather, it shines *through* it to provide hope and guidance. Christ, the Light of the World (cf. John 8:12), promises to lead us through the darkness, and—if we follow him unreservedly—to keep evil at bay, to even thwart it. As John the Baptist's father Zechariah prophesies in the *Benedictus* (Luke 1:67-79): "By the tender mercy of our God, the dawn from on high will break upon us, to give light to those who sit in darkness and in the shadow of death, to guide our feet into the way of peace."

Christmas reminds us to seek that light again, to follow it, to *become* that point of light along the dark and narrow path of life. Our rejoicing in the light that Christ provides should, like George Bailey, provide a beacon of hope for others on the same journey. We all must become the light that shines in the darkness. As Jesus told the disciples of his day (and ours), "You are the salt of the earth" and the "light of the world. . . . Let your light shine before others, so that they may see your good works and give glory to your Father in heaven" (Matthew 5:13,14,16).

A Savior is born for us from God's *zeal*, or passion, as Isaiah says (9:7). Interestingly, a few sentences after his account of the birth of Jesus, Luke tells us that the shepherds who had seen the light "went with *haste*" and found Mary, Joseph, and the infant Jesus lying in a manger (Luke 2:16). They were *eager* to find the source of the light, and after seeing Jesus, while expressing the zeal of God's love, they "returned, glorifying and praising God for all they had heard and seen" (Luke 2:20).

The light shining in the darkness of that first Christmas night transformed them, as it should with us today—and not just at Christmas, but throughout the year. St. Paul reminds us when he says that the "grace of God has appeared, bringing salvation to all, training us to renounce impiety and worldly passions, and in the present age to live lives that are self-controlled, upright, and godly" as we await the final coming of Christ (Titus 2:11-12). This is our baptismal call as Christians.

The darkness has not overcome us because God has stepped into it, has shown and given us the light, and because he leads us into the light for all eternity. As the Book of Revelation says:

*The home of God is among mortals. He will dwell with them; they will be his peoples, and God himself will be with them; he will wipe every tear from their eyes. Death will be no more; mourning and crying and pain will be no more, for the first things have passed away. They will see his face, and his name will be on their foreheads. And there will be no more night; they need no light of lamp or sun, for the Lord God will be their light, and they will reign for ever and ever.*

—Revelation 21:3-4; 22:4-5

# True Rest

"Lord, you have made us for yourself, and our heart is restless until it rests in you," St. Augustine prays in the opening lines of his *Confessions*. This famous quote sums up our relationship with God. Nothing but God alone satisfies the deepest longing within our hearts, a longing for reunion with our Creator. During this life, we often mistake this longing for something of much lesser value, and misplace the object of our hope. But deep down—whether we acknowledge it or not—we yearn for God, echoing the words of the Psalmist: "For God alone my soul waits in silence; from him comes my salvation" (Psalm 62:2).

Job's lament in the Old Testament is the same: "I am full of tossing until dawn" (Job 7:1-4, 6-7). He has lost everything of earthly value: his possessions, his family, and his health. Though he says he is "without hope," his very cry to God expresses hope. A hungry infant cries *expecting* to be heard and satisfied. True hopelessness is deathly silent. As St. Paul writes, "Who hopes for what is seen?" (Romans 8:24).

So, we are weak and weary, but we hope in God, who comes to meet us in the person of Christ. To the weak, he becomes weak, to win over the weak—just as St. Paul followed in his steps and modeled for us (cf. 1 Corinthians 9:22-23). Jesus took on our human weakness to give us strength, restore our hope, and provide the rest for which we long. It is for this purpose that he came into this world and continues to dwell in it through the Body of Christ, the Church, in which God the Father breathes the Holy Spirit. Just as with Simon's mother-in-law at the beginning of Mark's Gospel, Christ approaches us in Word and Sacrament, grasps us by the hand, and helps us up (Mark 1:29-39).

Later in Mark's Gospel (6:30-34), Jesus invites his disciples: "Come away to a deserted place all by yourselves and rest a while." The same invitation is extended to us, as well as to others *through* us. "Come to me, all you that are weary and are carrying heavy burdens, and I will give you rest," he says in Matthew's Gospel (11:28).

We may indeed lament along with Job, saying, "I am full of tossing until dawn." However, the word *dawn* is the key to that sentence. Dawn brings light, hope, and the promise of the Resurrection—new life. The dawn is none other than Christ himself—God Among Us. It is for him that our restless hearts long. Christ is our Light. "I am the light of the world," he tells us. "Whoever follows me will never walk in darkness but will have the light of life" (John 8:12).

In Mark 1:29-39, Jesus, *rising very early before dawn*, goes off to a deserted place to pray. If we read previous verses in the same chapter, it becomes clear that it is the day after the traditional Sabbath— Sunday, the day of the Resurrection to come. And what happens? Jesus is pursued to the deserted place, and when his disciples find him, they say, "Everyone is searching for you." Jesus responds: "Let us go on to the neighboring towns, so that I may proclaim the message there also; for that is what I came to do." He offers us rest, coming to meet us on the Day of Resurrection, giving us life by giving his very self. *God does this.* He is our rest.

This is the same message foretold and fulfilled throughout all of Scripture. It is the same simple message repeated in various forms on every page of this book. It is the same because it is true, Truth itself, and nothing but the Truth matters. And when we allow ourselves to discover and truly embrace that Truth, we become its stewards—just like St. Paul. To the weak, we become weak, to win over the weak (cf. 1 Corinthians 9:22-23).

When our hearts find rest in God alone, we discover renewed strength and purpose, arising like Simon's mother-in-law to serve those around us (Mark 1:30-31). In gratitude for what we have received, we then seek to provide rest and hope to others whose hearts are full of tossing until dawn. We search for Jesus in a deserted place, looking for the morning light of hope. Then, we arise to win over the weary of heart, becoming—like Christ—all things to all people for the sake of the gospel. ❧

# In the Desert

The significance of Mark's Gospel account of the temptation of Jesus and the beginning of his ministry (Mark 1:12-15) is best considered in light of what immediately precedes it (Mark 1:9-11)—and what the combined passages signify in the context of salvation history stretching back to the Creation and the Exodus.

In Genesis, the mighty wind of God's breath, or Spirit, moves over the dark and watery chaos to give shape and order to heaven and earth. Later, after God breathes the same life-giving spirit into the man he has formed in his own image from clay, Adam (*Adama* or "ground" in Hebrew) lives among the beasts in the perfectly ordered wilderness of Eden. We all know what happens shortly thereafter. Hundreds of years later, Moses leads God's chosen people out of slavery and into the desert on a journey to the Promised Land.

In Mark 1:9-11, Jesus emerges from his baptism in the watery chaos of the Jordan as the breath of God's Holy Spirit descends upon him in the form of a dove and the Father's voice announces him as Son of God. This is a *new* creation. In Mark 1:12-15, the same Spirit drives Jesus out into the desert or wilderness, where he lives among the wild beasts and is tempted by Satan. Here, we have a new exodus.

In the desert of the universal human journey, Jesus—God made man, the new Adam—encounters both good and evil, struggle, and temptation. But angels also minister to him, and he faithfully emerges from the battle we all fight to proclaim the gospel of God, and ultimately, to die on a cross and then rise again to new life.

The message is this: We are *not* alone! Emmanuel (God with us) has not left us to fend for ourselves, despite all indications to the contrary. Through the Church, his Spirit continues to reveal his presence, offer us new life, and lead us through the desert of struggle and temptation to the Promised Land. Along the way, angels minister to us.

Everyday details have eternal significance. The divine presence is everywhere. Every day offers a sacred way. "The time is fulfilled, and the kingdom of God has come near," Jesus says. "Repent [or turn toward God], and believe in the good news" (Mark 1:15).

So, for those of us who are baptized in the name of the Father, and the Son, and the Holy Spirit, the question we must ask ourselves is this:

*"Where am I in this picture?"* ♠

# Back to the Future

After predicting his passion and death and outlining the self-sacrificing conditions of authentic discipleship (cf. Mark 8:31-9:1), Jesus takes Peter, James, and John (three Apostles who will later take on important leadership roles in the Early Church) up a mountain. There, he is transfigured before them in a sight almost too wonderful to behold (cf. Mark 9:2-10). Also appearing with him are Elijah and Moses, representing the Prophets and the Law, which are fulfilled in the person of Christ, the Son of God (cf. Luke 24:44; 4:24).

Notice the distinct Trinitarian elements in Mark's account: three Apostles; Law, Prophets, and Fulfillment; and finally, God the Father, Son, and Holy Spirit. In a scene remarkably similar to that of the baptism of Jesus, a cloud descends, and from it a voice declares, "This is my Son, the Beloved; listen to him!" God reveals himself to the three Apostles, giving them a brief glimpse of Christ in his glory, and connecting his appearance with all that has happened before him throughout salvation history.

For the moment, Peter, James, and John are simply terrified and mystified. Later, after the Resurrection of Christ, the Ascension to God the Father, and the descent of the Holy Spirit at Pentecost, this will all make more sense to them as they begin their work of laying the Church's foundation.

Most interesting are three words at the beginning of the Gospel passage that are not actually read at Mass from the *Lectionary*: "Six days later. . ." *Six days after what?*

These three words tie together what follows—the Transfiguration—with what preceded it—the prediction of Jesus' passion and death, along with the costly demands of discipleship (which Peter, at least, didn't want to hear). So, *seven days* after Jesus lays it all on the line and tells his disciples what to realistically expect, *he reveals his glory.* The three future leaders of the Early Church are given a heavenly foretaste of what self-sacrifice in Christ, and through Christ, will mean for all disciples through all ages. In other words, after the harshness of what was told them six days earlier, *on the seventh day, they were given* **hope.**

And that is precisely what we celebrate every Sunday—the seventh day, and the beginning of all the days that follow. We celebrate the hope of the Resurrection that is ours in Christ, and we enter into God's rest. This was prefigured in Genesis' story of Creation: God "rested on the seventh day from all the work that he had done. So God blessed the seventh day and hallowed it" (Genesis 2:2-3). On the seventh day, we rest in our hope in the New Creation that comes to us through Christ. We are given a glimpse of the transfiguration that awaits all the faithful who deny themselves, take up their cross, and follow Jesus.

Truly, it is good for us to be here! Today, we behold the Resurrection and the Life, and know that whoever believes in him, even if he dies, will live, and that everyone who lives and believes in him will never die (cf. John 11:25-26).

So, as Jesus asks Martha in John 11:27, before raising her brother Lazarus from the dead: *"Do* **YOU** *believe this?"*

Let us listen to him. ✤

# Surprised by Hope

In the May 2, 2011, issue of the Jesuit weekly magazine, *America*, Dominican sister and New Testament professor Barbara E. Reid writes insightfully about Luke's Gospel story of the disciples on the road to Emmaus as a metaphor for the Christian virtue of hope. To illustrate her point, she quotes Vaclav Havel, the former president of the Czech Republic:

> *Hope is not the conviction*
> *that something will turn out well,*
> *but the certainty that something makes sense,*
> *regardless of how it turns out.*

Similarly, the Letter to the Hebrews (11:1) famously connects hope to the virtue of faith:

> *Faith is the assurance of things hoped for,*
> *the conviction of things not seen.*

The disciples on their way to Emmaus in Luke's Gospel (24:13-35) are unseeing. Things have not turned out well in their eyes. They are uncertain, unconvinced—*looking sad*, Luke tells us. They are walking *away* from Jerusalem, the city which just a week previous held so much promise for them, so much hope. "We had hoped. . . " they tell the stranger who appears at their side along the way.

They—just like each of us—are in need of the assurance that faith provides. The stranger listens. He understands. He journeys with them, interprets their doubts in the light of Scripture, and then stays with them, joins them at table. As he takes bread, says the blessing, breaks it, and gives it to them, their eyes are opened.

*It is Jesus!*

Now they are certain, convinced, joyful. Hearts burning within them, by faith they head back to Jerusalem, the city of hope, to share the good news.

These two disciples represent all Christians, then and now. We are a pilgrim people journeying in a time of "exile," as the First Letter of Peter (1:17-21) says. We are living in temporary exile from our true home, the heavenly Jerusalem, for which we strive by faith, in hope, and through the love burning within us.

Our encounter with the Risen Christ along the way is the source of our faith, hope, and love. He is all that makes sense, regardless of how anything else appears to turn out. Jesus transforms our doubt into faith. *He is never absent.* He makes himself present to us in Word and Sacrament during this time of our exile. He enlightens us, feeds us, and brings us together in his name.

Stay with us, Lord! ♣

# Ascension

**W**here is God in all this? It's a fair question, one we all ask at times in one way or another. It's a question we *should* ask, and which God *expects* us to ask. Faithful people *do* ask.

Ah, but we don't always listen for, or to, the answers, do we?

Some of the Mass readings offered for use in the celebration of the Solemnity of the Ascension of the Lord provide some insight (Acts 1:1-11; Ephesians 4:1-13; Mark 16:15-20). On the surface of things, it may seem as though after the Resurrection, Jesus appeared to some of his disciples, and then ascended into Heaven, where he remains today. We know he'll come back, but we don't know when, and he sure seems to be taking his time about it. So we just wait?

In one sense, yes; but in another, more important sense, no. The Kingdom of Heaven is both *now* and *not yet*. Like a seed planted in the spring, it has sprouted and spread during the long growing season (yes, along with all those nasty weeds and meddling pests!), but it has not yet reached the time of harvesting. It is here now, but has not yet *fully* arrived. And like any farmer, we have a part to play in how fruitful the harvest is. God supplies the sun, rain, and the mystery of germination, but we have to cultivate, plant, and prune. The latter is not possible without the former, but the farmer's toil is also necessary for the gift of redemption to bear fruit.

Like anything worth having, it requires some "elbow grease," but most of all, it involves a *choice*. As Jesus says in Mark 16:15-20, "The one who believes and is baptized will be saved; but the one who does not believe will be condemned." Each moment, we must choose, as the Letter to the Ephesians states, to "lead a life worthy of the calling" which you have received (Ephesians 4:1).

However, we are not alone. God does not stand off at a distance to simply watch us wallow in our collective, self-induced wretchedness and misery as we await the Second Coming. It may *seem* that way sometimes, but reality often eludes perception.

Rather, acting from an immense love we cannot begin to comprehend, the Creator of the Universe stooped down to lend a hand in the only way that makes sense. In the person of Christ, he took on himself the humanity we had disfigured by ill-advised choice—which inflicts all measure of the misery we experience in this world. Rather than coolly directing a way out from on high, he rolled up his sleeves and jumped into the fray with us. He doesn't just provide a solution; he enters the problem—*becomes* the problem. He transforms humanity from within, something like how a vaccine containing a virus is injected into the body to ward off more virulent strains.

*But if that's true, where is he? Things seem pretty awful. He seems absent. Maybe he was once here, but if he ascended, then we seem to be abandoned.*

Therein lies the mystery of the Cross. That's the *vaccine*—the Death, Resurrection, and Ascension of a God who became one of us to take us up, lift us up, to a Heaven which must *begin* here on Earth, within earthly things. We live in him, and he lives in us, his Body, which sanctifies the sufferings we endure in this world. The Church is that Body, mystically united to the One who awaits us and who is present to us (yes, amid all the weeds and pests).

But we are free to choose. No one's decision is forced. We do, however, have to bear the consequences of our choices, both individually and collectively. We're in this together. When one part of the Body is sick, the *whole* Body experiences it.

But the cure is at hand, and it—Jesus—is here. Largeness within smallness. Extraordinary within the ordinary.

*Where?*

He is present through the Holy Spirit, which he promises and bestows on all who believe, so that we, as his Body, may do his works—even greater works than Jesus did (cf. John 14:12)! "You will receive power when the Holy Spirit has come upon you; and you will be my witnesses . . . to the ends of the earth," Jesus said before his Ascension as recorded in the Acts of the Apostles. And in Mark's Gospel (16:20), he tells us, "Go into all the world and proclaim the good news to the whole creation."

With the promise of the Holy Spirit, which filled the Church at Pentecost, we have God among us in *greater measure* than the apostles did when they walked and talked with Jesus! We encounter him in prayer, in Scripture, in worship and praise, and in the sacraments—particularly the Eucharist. We encounter him in the practice of virtue, in the charity we express toward one another, in the compassion we show one another, the joy we share, and in the unity and peace for which we strive.

And we encounter him in our sorrows, our grief, doubt, pain, and confusion. In such moments, we call out all the more—we seek God all the more because we *have* him all the more. We meet him in the Cross that he shares with us, providing us with the way to Heaven through our earthly reality.

After Jesus ascended into Heaven, we are told in the last verse of Mark's Gospel, that he *worked with them*. From Heaven, through the Holy Spirit, he works with us, alongside us, within us, to lead us home for eternity.

*Where is God in all this?*

Where *isn't* he? As Ephesians 1:23 assures us: Christ "*fills all in all.*" In Heaven, and on Earth.

Now and forever. ♣

# "I Am with You Always"

If one were looking for a short, simple passage that synthesizes all of Scripture, summarizes Jesus' purpose for coming among us, and declares the mission of the Church, the conclusion of the Gospel of Matthew (28:16-20) would be an excellent choice.

Much of Scripture speaks of the establishment of the Kingdom of God in a manner that surpasses all human expectations (i.e. Acts 1:1-11 and Ephesians 1:17-23). The conclusion of Matthew's Gospel, in particular, portrays Jesus completely reclaiming a fallen world wounded by sin, and commissioning his weak, doubtful, and confused disciples to proclaim this message of hope to all peoples.

Can you imagine? These *eleven*, as Matthew points out (Judas having betrayed Jesus before his death), are unlearned men still stunned by Jesus' resurrection. They doubted, Matthew says. And they did more than that. These same men, while trying to follow Jesus, nonetheless were tripped up by human ambition, jealousy, selfishness, pride, misunderstanding, fear, and even denial of Christ. The first disciples were just as broken as we are!

Yet Jesus entrusts the Church to them—to *us*. We are to evangelize, celebrate the sacraments, teach one another, and live the gospel—but not all alone. "I am with you always, to the end of the age," Jesus says.

This powerful promise echoes throughout Scripture. It's there in Matthew's infancy narrative, recalling the words of the prophet Isaiah: "They shall name him Emmanuel, which means 'God is with us'" (cf. Matthew 1:23 and Isaiah 7:14). And it is there in 2 Chronicles 36:23, the very last words of the Hebrew Bible, when the earthly King Cyrus claims his dominion under God and links it to the temple in Jerusalem, urging the people, "Whoever is among you of all his people, may the Lord his God be with him!"

All this is tied together and fulfilled when Christ the True King ascends into Heaven with the Earth at his feet, and then at Pentecost sends the Holy Spirit to be with his first disciples—and *us* in the building up of God's heavenly Kingdom.

Whatever our trials and weaknesses, we are filled with hope because Christ is with us—to the ends of the earth, and to the end of the age. Amen. ♣

# Strength that Comes from God

How often have you received a word of encouragement at the precise moment at which you needed it? A phone call, an email, a "chance" encounter with a friend, the simple wisdom of an innocent child, or an inner epiphany of sorts that sheds new light on everything.

We've all received them at one time or another. Occasionally, such moments provide strength we did not realize we had, to accomplish something we would never have dreamed of previously. In the Book of Genesis (12:1-4a), the patriarch Abraham is called by God to leave everything behind to go somewhere else for a purpose yet to be revealed. But the command comes with a promise of untold blessing. So, by faith, Abraham sets out to accomplish by grace God's design for him.

Such a promise is revealed in Matthew's Gospel (17:1-9) as Jesus appears transfigured on the mountaintop to Peter, James, and John. Significantly, just before this scene, in Matthew's chapter 16, Jesus had begun to foretell his crucifixion and speak of the high cost of discipleship for anyone wishing to follow him. So, the Transfiguration is a moment of light, a word of encouragement to the same three apostles who will later be present during Jesus' agony in the garden of Gethsemane. After his death and resurrection, this moment of Transfiguration becomes a *source of hope and strength* in the disciples' mission of spreading the Gospel amid hardship and persecution.

As St. Paul says, "join with me in suffering for the gospel, relying on the power of God," because Jesus has "abolished death and brought life and immortality to light through the gospel" (2 Timothy 1:8b-10).

Like Abraham, God has designs for each one of us, and it is by his grace that we **CAN** accomplish them! ❧

# Where Is God?

*Out of the depths I cry to you, O Lord.*
　　　　　　　　　—Psalm 130

*Why do you sleep, O Lord?*
　　*Awake, do not cast us off forever!*
*Why do you hide your face?*
　　*Why do you forget our affliction and oppression?*
　　　　　　　　　—Psalm 44

All of us experience periods of spiritual dryness or desolation, times when God seems distant or absent altogether. And when we or others are suffering physically or emotionally, we are bound to cry out as did the author of the psalms above. It is part of the human experience.

Yet, if there is no hope, why do we cry out, and to whom?

The absence of hope brings death. Hope in the midst of suffering can redeem it and restore life in ways we cannot begin to imagine. God is not distant or absent from our lives. If that were the case, we would simply cease to be.

This is a theologically rich topic. Acres of text stretching back to the gospels and beyond have explored this mystery, so central to the Christian faith. As Christians, we believe Christ gives our suffering— even our doubts—meaning and purpose by taking on our humanity and dying on the cross, where the Second Person of the Holy Trinity himself cried out, "My God, my God, why have you forsaken me?" (Psalm 22; Matthew 27:46; Mark 15:34).

But it doesn't end there. Eventually, the darkness of Good Friday gives way to the light and life of Resurrection. "I am the resurrection and the life," Jesus says in John 11:25. In the words of the French poet Paul Claudel, "Jesus did not come to remove suffering, or to explain it, but to fill it with his *presence*" (emphasis is mine). God is with us in Christ—in Word and Sacrament, and in the life of the Church, the Body of Christ.

And he is with us in the very depths of our hearts, through which he breathes his life-giving Spirit. Every heartbeat testifies to God's abiding presence in our lives, which he created. And every cry coming from the depths of our hearts not only reaches him, but beats in unison with that Spirit within us.

The truth of the matter is that sometimes things seem distant because they are so *close*. Can you appreciate a Monet with your nose pressed up against the painting? Can you see the misplaced glasses you're searching for perched atop your head? "What no eye has seen, nor ear heard, nor the human heart conceived, what God has prepared for those who love him" (1 Corinthians 2:9).

And, of course, the psalms are a perfect way to pray this mystery in unison with Christ. As the Church prays at Compline in the evenings:

*Those who love me, I will deliver;*
*I will protect those who know my name.*
*When they call to me, I will answer them;*
*I will be with them in trouble,*
*I will rescue them and honor them.*
*With long life I will satisfy them*
*and show them my salvation.*
—Psalm 91:14-16

*Love*

# Lover of Souls

Jesus was passing through Jericho. The tax collector Zacchaeus, we are told in Luke's Gospel (19:1-10), wants to see him, but is prevented by his stature. Luke presents this as a physical limitation, but one wonders if his "spiritual stature" also was lacking in some way—or if his deficient "stature" as perceived by his fellow citizens prompted *them* to exclude him. After all, the text states that "he was trying to see who Jesus was, but on account of the crowd he could not." Perhaps it was a little of both—he was wealthy and a chief tax collector, attributes which imply greed, deceit, and the scorn that would have been directed his way as a result.

Whatever the case may be, Zacchaeus had genuine desire in his heart to see the Lord. So he did the only thing he could—he climbed a tree! The scene is an amusing one. When Jesus approaches, he looks up at Zacchaeus in the tree above him and says, "Zacchaeus, hurry and come down; for I must stay at your house today." And so the stature-challenged man (in whatever sense that applies) "hurried down and was happy to welcome him," Luke says.

Jesus literally invites himself to the home of Zacchaeus. Isn't it surprising that Jesus would do this? After all, the two did not know one another, and surely there were plenty of more "upstanding" citizens in the surrounding crowd with whom Jesus could have stayed. Besides, Luke makes it clear that Jesus had every intention of passing through Jericho without stopping. But he *does* stop, and he tells Zacchaeus to come down from the sycamore tree because "I must stay at your house today." He hadn't even been asked!

Overwhelmed with joy, Zacchaeus—although loathed as the wealthy tax collector and "outsider" that he was—receives Jesus into his home (*or was it his heart?*). Meanwhile, Luke reports, "all who saw it began to grumble and said, 'He has gone to be the guest of one who is a sinner.'" In self-righteous horror, Jericho's more respectable citizenry is shocked—and likely more than a little jealous! But as Jesus declares earlier in Luke's Gospel, "I have come to call not the righteous but sinners to repentance" (5:32), and also at the closing of this particular passage in Luke: "The Son of Man came to seek out and to save the lost" (19:10).

With the foot of Jesus in the door, so to speak, Zacchaeus is moved to repent and atone for his sins, and so Jesus tells him, "Today salvation has come to this house."

It does not take much for God's mercy to enter into our lives. All that is necessary is a small opening—often arriving in surprising ways and at unexpected times—and a willing reception. God will do the rest. God is good, and all that he has created is good, as the Book of Wisdom reminds us: The Lord "is merciful to all, for you can do all things, and you overlook people's sins, so that they may repent. For you love all things that exist, and detest none of the things that you have made, for you would not have made anything if you had hated it . . . You spare all things, for they are yours, O Lord, who love the living" (11:23-24, 26).

So he pursues any who have gone astray "little by little" (cf. Wisdom 12:2) and slips into any opening he finds. *Why?* Because you have been fashioned by the Lord and lover of souls.

Whatever your spiritual stature may be—real or perceived—ask yourself: *Where might God be inviting himself into my life?* 🌰

# This Is BIG

God's love for humanity is so big, so immense, and so high, that he makes himself small, insignificant, and low to lift us up. In John's Gospel (13:1-15), we are told that Jesus, the Word made Flesh, at supper before the feast of Passover, "got up from the table, *took off his outer robe, and tied a towel around himself,*" and then began washing the disciples' feet.

God stoops down, literally taking the form of a slave, to cleanse those enjoying the banquet with him. In doing this, he strips himself of divine privilege and wraps himself in the towel of servile humanity. However, Jesus does *much more* than simply wash the disciples' feet. This action symbolically illustrates what he will do in reality on Good Friday, when he will be stripped of his garments and nailed to a cross to cleanse and free humanity—just as the slaughtered lamb at Passover saved the children of Israel in Egypt. In doing so, he offers all a seat at the heavenly banquet (cf. Exodus 12:1-8, 11-14; 1 Corinthians 11:23-26).

All this, of course, echoes the famous Christian hymn in Paul's letter to the Philippians (2:7-8):

*He emptied himself,*
*taking the form of a slave,*
*being born in human likeness.*
*And being found in human form,*
*he humbled himself*
*and became obedient to the point of death—*
*even death on a cross.*

With this posture in mind, during the celebration of the Evening Mass of the Lord's Supper on Holy Thursday, we recall in a special way God's self-sacrificing love for us as we commemorate his Passion, Death, and Resurrection. God stoops down to us, allows himself to be broken and shared among us, so that we who are so broken may together become the whole Christ, blessed and shared with all.

Like Peter, who at first didn't allow Jesus to wash his feet, we who are so small want a God *bigger* than us—perhaps because that would "let us off the hook" in so many respects (because if God is not human, then we humans certainly cannot be expected to model the divine!). Though God *is* bigger, he *becomes* small enough to be placed in our hands and on our tongues in the Eucharist. Kneeling before his disciples at the Last Supper, stripped of all dignity on the cross, and in the form of bread and wine in the Eucharist, the Son of God gives us his very self so that we may live in him and he may live in us.

Then, Jesus asks us as he did the apostles:

*"Do you know what I have done to you?"*

Our honest answer must be: *"No, not really."*

However, our honest prayer can be: *"Not yet. Wash me."*

Sometimes growing in spiritual maturity means merely recognizing our capacity for it—and being small enough to ask for it. Stooped down, broken and shared in love for the life of the world, we are raised as the Body of Christ higher than we ever imagined. ♠

# God's Passionate Embrace

Can you imagine God as your passionate Lover? One who recognizes your long loneliness as a human being, and who longs intensely to bridge the chasm of fear between the human and divine, drawing you into the loving presence of the Divine? Can you imagine being immersed in God's passionate embrace—not in the lascivious sense we so often consciously imagine or fall prey to in today's sex-obsessed culture, but in the honest, committed, and chaste sense of generously responding to a spouse's absolute tenderness with total trust, peace, joy, comfort, and love?

Well, try!

Does such an image shock you? Does it sound too erotic? Well it is—it is holy *eros*! Yes, it is a very powerful and provocative idea, but it is not a new one by any stretch of the imagination, and it is one of which we all need to be reminded.

Scripture and our Christian tradition present us with many images of God's everlasting love for us. The list is too long to recite, but Scripture in various places presents God as a loving parent, disciplinarian, sibling, teacher, shepherd, healer, and friend, among other things. In addition, it seems that we typically have no trouble focusing on the image of God as the Supreme Being who judges and punishes.

None of these images, presented by God through his Word, are wrong in and of themselves. However, there is another that encompasses all of these but which we typically fail to recognize or respond to. And I would suggest that it is the *primary* way in which God wishes to relate to each and every one of us.

This is the image of God as a *passionate lover*, a God who *really digs you*, and a God who wants absolutely nothing but to have that passionate love reciprocated. Just as two spouses unite in the total gift of self, God wishes to embrace each one of us, and remain that way for eternity in supreme joy and happiness.

Like marriage, it is a covenant relationship. It is an erotic love (energized with individual desire, but disciplined and purified) that leads us to *agape* (self-giving love directed outward to encompass and generate life among all). *Agape* is totally selfless, only seeking the good of the beloved, and is most fully expressed in the love shared among the three Persons of the Holy Trinity, of which Christians are invited to share (cf. John 13:34-35).

As the *Cathechism of the Catholic Church* states:

God who created man out of love also calls him to love—the fundamental and innate vocation of every human being. For man is created in the image and likeness of God, who is himself love. Since God created him man and woman, *their mutual love becomes an image of the absolute and unfailing love with which God loves man*. It is good, very good, in the Creator's eyes (*CCC*, 1604, *emphasis added*).

As anyone who has had an honest, committed, and chaste relationship knows, the most passionate lover sharing him or herself in this way also displays many of the other qualities above that are associated with God. The truth is that God is beyond our imagining. No image suffices. God is all of these and much, *much* more.

However, if one takes a step back from Scripture and tradition with an honest view toward the whole, this is what emerges: *God is Love* (cf. 1 John 4:8, 16). These three words express it all—creation, redemption, resurrection, and everlasting life. Scripture, tradition, and all of salvation history up to this very moment are chapters in an epic love story of a God who pursues us with almost insane jealousy in order to draw us into a love beyond our imagination.

This nuptial relationship that we are called to share with God—and through God, with one another—is expressed both implicitly and explicitly throughout Scripture. In that regard, the following passages are just a few of the many worth meditating on: Exodus 6:7; The Book of Ruth; Psalm 45; Isaiah 62:5; Hosea 2:19-20; John 17:26; and Revelation 19:1-9.

But the most prominent illustration of this within the canon is the Song of Solomon, which is in everybody's Bible but (I'm willing to bet) rarely read. It is a beautiful love poem with a strikingly erotic tone. God is the Bridegroom, and God's people are the Bride. Here are a few lines:

**BRIDEGROOM:**

*How fair and pleasant you are,*
    *O loved one, delectable maiden!*
*You are stately as a palm tree,*
    *and your breasts are like its clusters.*
*I say I will climb the palm tree*
    *and lay hold of its branches.*
*O may your breasts be like clusters of the vine,*
    *and the scent of your breath like apples,*
*and your kisses like the best wine*
    *that goes down smoothly,*
    *gliding over lips and teeth.*


**BRIDE:**

*I am my beloved's,*
    *and his desire is for me.*
*Come, my beloved,*
    *let us go forth into the fields,*
    *and lodge in the villages;*
*let us go out early to the vineyards,*
    *and see whether the vines have budded,*
*whether the grape blossoms have opened*
    *and the pomegranates are in bloom.*
*There I will give you my love.*
*The mandrakes give forth fragrance,*
    *and over our doors are all choice fruits,*
*new as well as old,*
    *which I have laid up for you, O my beloved.*
        —Song of Solomon 7:6-13

*Whew!* Once I was in a class on Human Sexuality and Christian Maturity, and one of the students, after hearing a passage read aloud like this exclaimed, *"That's* in the Bible?!"

Yes, that's in the Bible, and for good reason. In poetic fashion, it describes God's relationship with his beloved people, who are increasingly drawn into spiritual union with the Lord through the bond of perfect love. In Christian tradition, the Song of Solomon has been interpreted on several levels—among them, as a vivid illustration of the collective union between Christ and his people (the Church), and as one typifying the union between God and the individual soul.

Saints—doctors of the Church—have written beautiful commentaries on the *Song of Solomon.* St. Bernard of Clairvaux and St. Francis de Sales come immediately to mind. Others have contributed poetic meditations in the same vein, such as St. Teresa of Avila and St. John of the Cross. Theirs was a passionate love for God, who loved them passionately, and sometimes the writings of these saints expressed this in erotic terms.

In his encyclical *Deus Caritas Est (God Is Love),* Pope Emeritus Benedict XVI boldly declared that God's love is personal:

> God loves, and his love may certainly be called *eros,* yet it is also totally *agape.* The prophets, particularly Hosea and Ezekiel, described God's passion for his people using boldly erotic images (*Deus Caritas Est,* 9).

In their book *Holy Eros: Pathways to a Passionate God,* James D. and Evelyn Whitehead write:

> This is an *eros* known through and beyond sexual arousal; its vital energy courses through the world, enlivening and healing human hearts. Experienced as affection and also as compassion, in desire and also in hope, *eros* becomes ever more generous as it folds into that most capacious love described in the Bible as *agape.*

I wonder why it surprises us, makes us so uncomfortable, to be told so explicitly of God's intensely passionate love for us? And yet it does—despite its solid roots in Scripture and tradition. For thousands of years, God's people, generally speaking, have been fearful of intimacy with God. Yielding to such fear has resulted in increasingly horrifying manifestations of human sin and pain. Yet, God still pursues us with steadfast love, hoping we will all one day realize that a person will only love truly when he or she is truly loved.

As philosopher Charles Taylor states in *Holy Eros*:

> We have to recover a sense of the link between erotic desire and the love of God, which lies deep in the Biblical traditions, whether Jewish or Christian, and find new ways of giving expression to this. . . . This terribly fraught area in Western Christendom, where the sexual meets the spiritual, urgently awaits discovery of new paths to God.

In Matthew's Gospel (14:22-33), Jesus walks on the stormy Sea of Galilee when his disciples, being tossed about by the waves, spot him from their boat. They are terrified. And he says to them: "Take heart, it is I; do not be afraid." Longing to be with Jesus on the water, Peter calls out to him. "Come," Jesus responds. So Peter gets out of the boat and miraculously begins walking on the water toward Jesus—until his fear returns and gets the best of him. He begins sinking, but Jesus catches him, draws him up safely out of the water, and returns with him to the boat.

The stormy seas of life frighten us as well, and despite our long loneliness as human beings, we are afraid to bridge the chasm of fear between us and God. Yet Jesus beckons from the turbulent and dreadful waters, "Do not be afraid. Come." God longs to draw us into his presence with the passion of a lover, but will not force us to do anything against our will. We are invited to step out of the boat, but if we begin to sink, God's arms will catch us. And if we won't—or can't—"step out of the boat" as the other disciples could not, God comes to us. We are invited to respond to the Divine Spouse's absolute tenderness with total trust, peace, joy, comfort, and love.

At some point, of course—whether we are single, married, or in religious life—we must not only chastely reciprocate God's passionate love for us in the manner suitable for our state in life, but *also* get out of the boat. Then, we must help others bridge that chasm of fear separating them from the love of God. Like God, we must be willing to approach the fearful soul with a smile, and through self-sacrificing service, share the supreme happiness and joy flowing from God's passionate love.

But this cannot be done until we *ourselves* accept the embrace of God—as Passionate Lover. ♣

# Polishing with Love

*If anyone is detected in a transgression,*
*you who have received the Spirit*
*should restore such a one*
*in a spirit of gentleness.*

—Galatians 6:1

We become persons—the true persons God created us to be in the image of the Holy Trinity, who is One God in Three Persons—in relationship with others. Our destinies are intertwined, whether we can see it or not, believe it or not. We are interdependent, particularly so as Christians.

Recognizing that is one thing. Living it is another. It is not easy.

When I first came to the monastery, I was talking with Br. Martin one day, and he compared living in community (in our case, a monastic community) with a big revolving mixer filled with many stones. Some of these stones are big, some small. Each has a different shape, color, and texture, and some are quite jagged. A wonderful thing happens as the mixer is turned, and all those stones begin scraping and scuffing one another. Over time, they become smooth and round and polished—a few may even become sparkling. This occurs (hopefully) by the grace of God working through our relationships with one another.

In light of Scripture, as a Christian community witnessing to the world, we must polish one another and the world at large, but this must be understood correctly. The Church is in the business of saving *souls*, not in preserving its own life within contemporary social, economic, or political realms. The Body of Christ does not exist for its own welfare, but for that of *souls*—all souls, throughout the world, for all time. Anything else ultimately corrupts and compromises the Church's spiritual mission (though God is capable of making "all things work together for good," as Romans 8:28 states).

Ironically, those who lose sight of this—attempting to turn the revolving mixer to their own beat—put their *own* souls at risk. "Those who want to save their life will lose it, and those who lose their life for my sake will save it," Jesus says (Luke 9:24; similar passages are found in all four gospels). Fundamentalism, whatever its form (and every "camp" has it to some degree) has never ultimately succeeded throughout the course of human history, and has often led to unspeakable crimes against humanity.

All of this is not genuine fraternal correction, the loving care of souls, as many passages in Scripture exhort us to demonstrate (i.e., Ezekiel 33:7-9; Romans 13:8-10; and Matthew 18:15-20). Turning the revolving mixer to one's own beat (or the beat of a particular camp) without charity and care of souls as its ultimate end is the absolute worst sin of all—pride, the downfall of our first parents.

Yes, as Ezekiel says in the passage cited above, we are each responsible for warning sinners and helping them turn to God. But in Matthew's Gospel, Jesus lays out a very measured, practical, and pastoral approach. In the occasion of sin (and he was talking about serious sin, not minor annoyances, offended sensibilities, or ultimately trivial disagreements), we are to take a brother or sister aside *privately* and speak with him or her about it. Grievances aren't to be aired publicly or by means of gossip. If that doesn't work, Jesus, says, bring a couple of others along—a firmer approach, what we would today call an "intervention." Last of all, if nothing else works, the matter is to be brought to the attention of the entire community.

Implied throughout is the call for prayer, for "where two or three are gathered in my name, I am there among them." It is also significant that following this Gospel passage in Matthew is the parable of the unforgiving servant, who is punished for his lack of compassion, patience, and mercy when he had been forgiven a far greater amount (Matthew 18:21-35). In other words, we all fall short of God's grace, and we must always keep that in mind, whether a fellow sinner repents or not.

I had an uncle (God, rest his soul) who loved to collect seemingly ordinary rocks and then cut, shape, and polish them into decorative works of beauty. He had his own shop filled with rocks and tools, and he gave his finished pieces to family members and friends. My uncle was able to see the hidden beauty within each rock, lovingly draw it out, and make it sparkle. There were no sledgehammers in his workshop. He polished with love.

Public accusation, rebuke, and humiliation seem to be increasingly in vogue these days—from both the left and right, and everywhere in-between, whether it's in the Church or the world at large. It's become quite wearisome, and is, quite frankly, the lazy way out. It is applying a sledgehammer with one ear-splitting blow rather than a polishing cloth privately and quietly over many hours, even days or weeks. In one case, the aim is really only to prove that might is right, and to prove the other wrong. In the latter case, something much deeper and longer-lasting is at stake—gently drawing out the reality of another's inner Truth, with tenderness and patience.

My uncle—and he was no pushover—*cared* for his rocks, and the people who would enjoy them. The sledgehammer wants only to drive home a point for its own sake. Both may have good intentions or even valid motivations, but ultimately the sledgehammer seeks its own life, while the polishing cloth seeks life at its own expense—as it polishes, the cloth ultimately wears away.

We are responsible for one another's salvation, yes, but with a view toward the genuine welfare of the other—not for our own welfare, nor for the mere sake of "winning an argument." As St. Paul says: "*Love* is the fulfilling of the law" (Romans 13:10).

This is the way we really and truly sparkle. ♠

# God Is Generously Unfair

S ometimes God offends human reason, and he means to do so. When we hear the parable from Matthew's Gospel of the workers in the vineyard (20:1-16a), it is natural for us to be just as offended as those laborers hired to work in the vineyard at the very beginning of the day. They receive the payment promised to them, but expect more for bearing the day's burden and heat when they see that the late arrivals are granted the same reward.

If we are honest, we may experience a similar reaction when we hear Luke's Gospel account of the repentant criminal crucified alongside Jesus. He is promised entry into Paradise, the Kingdom of God, despite a life of sin (Luke 23:39-43).

That is *unfair*!

If you've ever worked with someone who receives the same pay but seems to get away with doing far less than you, then you know how the first laborers in today's Gospel feel. According to human standards of justice and reason, it is totally unacceptable.

But that is precisely the point. As God says through the words of the prophet Isaiah, "My thoughts are not your thoughts, nor are your ways my ways. For as the heavens are higher than the earth, so are my ways higher than your ways and my thoughts than your thoughts" (55:8-9). God is generous in forgiving beyond all human expectation or sense of justice. As the landowner (i.e., God) says in Matthew's account of Jesus' parable, "Are you envious because I am generous?" (20:15).

Biblical texts such as this (Matthew's parable of the unforgiving servant in 18:21-35 is another example), challenge us to consider something crucial to our very salvation: Do we—deep down—consider ourselves *worthy* of the Kingdom of God? Do we place demands on God's mercy? Do we who are "good" feel entitled to God's mercy, to entrance into the Kingdom, becoming envious when someone "less worthy" in our eyes receives the same "reward"?

Or are we simply grateful for and responsive to God's mercy—toward all, even the most "undeserving"?

The Kingdom of God cannot be earned—by *anyone*. We know this, profess this, but often secretly wish and act as if it were not true, especially in today's culture of rampant entitlement.

This is a very persistent theme throughout the gospels. Consider, for example, the parable that is well-known as "The Story of the Prodigal Son" (Luke 15:11-32). The elder son remains faithful and loyal to his father, while his younger brother acts shamelessly, disgracing his father's name. But the younger son repents (even if it is imperfect, self-centered repentance), comes home, and is joyfully greeted by his father, who then throws him a big party!

That is unfair! And the elder son tells his father so. The father (i.e., God) tells his elder son (i.e., you and me) essentially the same thing as the landowner in Matthew 20: "You are always with me, and all that is mine is yours." He, too, was invited to join in the feast—to enter the Kingdom of God, as it were. But his own resentment and envy prevented him from crossing the threshold. That was his choice, not that of the father, who begged him to put his anger aside and come in along with everyone else to celebrate and enjoy the feast.

What God imparts to us throughout his Word is that the bold sinner who genuinely repents is much closer to the Kingdom of God than those of us who "play it safe" and measure our worthiness against that of others. He asks us to accept the fact that the Good Shepherd will relentlessly pursue *one* lost sheep out of a flock of 100 to bring it safely back to the fold, where he invites us all (cf. Luke 15:3-7).

God's love is *radical*. It is *relentless*. Just as the landowner in Matthew's Gospel went out not once, not twice, but five times throughout the course of the day to bring more people into his vineyard, so God pursues each one of us. He is *crazy in love* with us, and wants us to share in his joy and love for us, to come to the banquet, to enter the sheepfold, to go into his vineyard, to cross the threshold of the Kingdom—they all mean the same thing.

God's love also is *absurdly abundant, excessively extravagant,* and *garishly generous.* His kisses are wet and sloppy (cf. Luke 15:20)!

Because of all this, God's love is unfair according to our human standards of measuring up. The last will be first, and the first will be last (cf. Matthew 20:16). Those left standing outside the Kingdom of God are there through their own choice.

So we each need to reflect on the question from Matthew's Gospel:

*"Are you envious because I am generous?"*

If we truly accept God's lavish generosity toward ourselves and others, then—and only then—we can live as St. Paul implores: "Live your life in a manner worthy of the gospel of Christ" (Philippians 1:27). This gospel is one of generosity. Let us take what is ours through God's generosity, and live it just as unfairly. ♠

# What Is a "Good" Christian?

In his book *Falling Upward: A Spirituality for the Two Halves of Life*, Richard Rohr states something very simply that is integral to the message of the gospel and so obvious, but something many of us fail to grasp (and I count myself one in that number). This is what he says:

> Jesus is never upset at sinners;
> he is only upset with people
> who do not think they are sinners!

Well, *duh*! We all know *that*!

But I wonder if we really do. Do we really believe, on one hand, that if we have sinned but have a change of heart and genuinely seek reconciliation and a firm purpose of amendment, that we *are* truly forgiven? We are cut free—forever, even though odds are we will sin again, and God knows that we will.

Do we really believe, on the other hand (and more pertinent to our discussion here), that this very same generous, even unfair offer of mercy is extended to *everyone* around us? In other words, do we sometimes unfairly judge others, placing ourselves above them, and primarily consider their shortcomings without regard to our own? Are we among those who do not think ourselves sinners (though we clearly are)?

In Jesus' related parables in Matthew's Gospel of the workers in the vineyard (20:1-16a) and the two sons commissioned by their father (21:28-32), the point is made that latecomers, sinners, the ones who initially refuse to do the will of God but who eventually have a change of heart, will enter the Kingdom of God. Meanwhile, the early arrivals, those who consider themselves upstanding religious and good Christians who say they believe and promise to act as believers, but who do not actually do so, may just find themselves outside the Kingdom of God. As Jesus tells the religious leaders in Matthew 21:31, "Tax-collectors and the prostitutes are going into the kingdom of God ahead of you."

It is worth nothing that this passage from Matthew comes shortly after Jesus' entry into Jerusalem, where he knows he will be put to death. One of his first actions in Jerusalem is to reclaim his Father's house, clearing out the temple area and declaring, "My house shall be called a house of prayer; but you are making it a den of robbers" (Matthew 21:13). This did not sit well with the religious leaders of Jerusalem, and they began questioning Jesus' authority. In response, Jesus relates the parable of the two sons commissioned to go to work in their father's vineyard. The first refuses to go, but changes his mind and does. The second says he will go, but he doesn't.

What Jesus is effectively saying is this: "I'm not interested in lip service and empty ritual for ritual's sake. I am interested in true, deep conversion of heart—in both worship and daily lives that demonstrate your belief in me."

Matthew's parable of the two sons also echoes the well-known story in Luke's Gospel (18:9-14) of the Pharisee (i.e., upstanding religious) and the tax collector (i.e., the repentant sinner) who both went into the temple area to pray. The Pharisee speaks this prayer: "God, I thank you that I am not like other people: thieves, rogues, adulterers, or even like this tax-collector . . ." Meanwhile, the tax collector simply bows his head in humility and says, "God, be merciful to me a sinner!" The latter, Jesus said, went home justified, not the former.

If we are completely honest with ourselves, there is a little of both the Pharisee and the tax collector in each of us. If we recognize that and assume the humble posture of the tax collector, then we are like the first son in Matthew's Gospel—the one who at first refuses to do his father's will, but then changes his mind, and therefore is allowed entrance into the Kingdom of God. However, if we assume the posture of an "upstanding" Christian, paying mere lip service like the second son, and like the Pharisee thanking God that we are "not like other people," then we are in for a *very* harsh surprise at the Last Judgment.

Satan, you see, doesn't necessarily want Christians to become atheists. He wants us to become Pharisees. That is why we must, as St. Paul says, strive daily to have the same mind "that was in Christ Jesus, who, though he was in the form of God, did not regard equality with God as something to be exploited (Philippians 2:5-6). ♠

# God's Zealous Love

The *American Heritage Dictionary* defines zeal as "enthusiastic devotion to a cause, ideal, or goal, and tireless diligence in its furtherance." It might also be said that zeal is simply love that stops at nothing.

As Jesus cleared the Jerusalem temple (cf. John 2:13-25) of those profiting from religion at the expense of the poor who sought only entrance into a true relationship with God, the disciples were reminded of Psalm 69: "Zeal for your house will consume me." They recognized at some level (though still not fully understanding) that the zealous love of God stops at nothing in claiming God's "house" for himself and his beloved people with whom he wishes to dwell. He wants to be alone with us, to have our undivided attention, and he is not polite in clearing the room to make this happen.

Within a generation after this episode, the Jerusalem temple was destroyed by Roman authorities while Jesus' risen body had ascended to his Father's house in Heaven. After the Resurrection, the disciples recalled that during Jesus' cleansing of the temple, he had said, "Destroy this temple, and in three days I will raise it up." Their understanding of Jesus' purpose then came into fuller view, and they realized that he was speaking of the "temple of his body."

God's zeal for his people strives to drive away all that prevents them from entering into a true relationship with him, so much so that he claims each person's heart for himself. He destroys our "false temples" and raises instead the Body of Christ, of which we are all members as baptized Christians, to be with him in Heaven. The "temple" of Jesus' body also belongs to each one of us because he has invited us in. There, he desires to dwell within the inner room of our hearts, just as the Holy Spirit filled the Upper Room and descended on the apostles at Pentecost.

As Paul says, "You are God's temple and God's Spirit dwells in you" (1 Corinthians 3:16 and 6:19).

So, we must ask ourselves, do we share God's zeal for his temple, which is our body within the Body of Christ? Have we allowed the "inner room" of our hearts to be claimed by Jesus? What is being "bought and sold" there that needs to be driven out, so that God's Spirit may dwell in you?

Let us recall that God's zealous love for us stops at absolutely nothing. We have only to let it consume us. ♠

# Great Love or Little?

*Her sins, which were many, have been forgiven;*
*hence, she has shown great love.*
*But the one to whom little is forgiven, loves little.*

—Luke 7:47

I n Luke's account of the sinful woman being forgiven (7:36-50), Jesus connects forgiveness with love. The woman who enters the house of the Pharisee to weep at Jesus' feet scandalizes everyone else by her mere presence. In *their* eyes, she is a sinner. She is an intruder—an uninvited guest. And yet, Jesus tells them all that because the woman's many sins have been forgiven, she shows great love.

Paradoxically, love is something that the law-abiding Pharisee and his guests lack. They are not bad people. In fact, in today's world, they would be considered upstanding citizens, parishioners, or members of the congregation. They follow and uphold the Law. They do what is right and just. In them there is no wrong—but to a prideful fault. Really, what need do they have for a Messiah? They have made *themselves* like God—the sin which led to the fall of our first parents (cf. Genesis 3:5) and made the world the broken place it is today.

And that is Jesus' point altogether. We cannot truly love unless we've been forgiven, and to be forgiven means acknowledging our weaknesses, limitations, and our sins—which *every* human being has in abundance by definition. It means being honest with God, with ourselves, and with others about who we really are. It is true humility. Mercy, after all, triumphs over judgment (cf. James 2:13).

For this reason, Jesus says to the Pharisee and his guests: "The one to whom little is forgiven, loves little." And to the woman, he says, "Your faith has saved you; go in peace."

# Peace and Joy

# Worry Not, Lilies of the Field

*Consider the lilies of the field, how they grow;*
*they neither toil nor spin, yet I tell you, even Solomon*
*in all his glory was not clothed like one of these.*
—Matthew 6:28-29

In 1988, jazz artist Bobby McFerrin's *a cappella* song "Don't Worry, Be Happy" soared to the top of the charts and eventually won a Grammy Award. The song became a cultural phenomenon, and its lyrics were widely quoted (sincerely or ironically) in everyday conversation, on T-shirts, on television, and even in political campaigns. Somehow, the expression—based on a longer maxim by the late Indian mystic Meher Baba—had tapped into what humanity deeply longs for—peace.

In Matthew's Gospel (6:24-34), Jesus clearly says several times over that we are not to worry. "Can any of you by worrying add a single hour to your span of life?" he admonishes. Throughout the gospels, he tells his disciples many times, "Do not be afraid." Yet, worrying is what many of us do best, and hearing messages like this can pile guilt on top of our anxiety because we know that we *should* have more trust in God.

Jesus, though, is not denying our legitimate concern for human needs, but rather is admonishing us to stop being so preoccupied with our wealth to the point that it enslaves us and deprives others. "You cannot serve God and wealth [or *mammon* in some translations]," Jesus tells us (Matthew 6:27).

*Webster's New World College Dictionary* defines mammon as "riches regarded as an object of worship and greedy pursuit." What's really at stake is not genuine concern for our daily bread, but rather an *attachment* to material wealth and comfort that supplants our reliance on God, who *is* our Daily Bread.

It is interesting to note that while Jesus calls God Father, the prophet Isaiah portrays God as a mother at one point: "Can a woman forget her nursing child, or show no compassion for the child of her womb? Even these may forget, yet I will not forget you" (Isaiah 49:15). Perhaps the point is that we should approach God more as a loving parent who both cares and provides for us rather than merely as a benefactor. When we embrace that sort of loving, trusting relationship, then we become true "servants of Christ and stewards of God's mysteries" (1 Corinthians 4:1), and we will find the peace of Christ that the world cannot provide. As Jesus told his disciples elsewhere: "Peace I leave with you; my peace I give to you. I do not give to you as the world gives. Do not let your hearts be troubled, and do not let them be afraid" (John 14:27).

Be happy, don't worry! ♠

# He Is Our Peace

Yes, the world is full of evil. We are divided, scattered, misled, untended, separated from one another and from our Creator. Sin, sweat, and sorrow plague us individually and socially. This has been the case for centuries upon centuries, and will continue to be the case as long as human beings inhabit the earth. We are utterly reprehensible. Who would love us?

*God would—and does.*

We do well to meditate on Scripture's presentation of Christ as the Good Shepherd, who comes among us to gather us back to himself, to guide us, care for us, and to reconcile us with God and one another. As the Letter to the Ephesians states, "He is our peace," putting our enmity to death by the cross on which he suffered and died (2:13-18). God sacrifices his very self for our salvation because there is no other way to reverse the Fall. Jesus sucks up all that is hideous about humanity into his sinless being, *becoming sin itself* (cf. 2 Corinthians 5:21). Then he exterminates it through his death—offering us everlasting hope through the Resurrection.

This is what he offers us—a free, immeasurable, unattainable gift. It is ours to accept or refuse; and if we choose to accept it, then we must live it daily by our own crosses, giving away our own lives out of love for God and one another—usually in small ways, but sometimes in much more significant fashion.

The key to understanding all this and making it a part of us is the utter compassion Jesus demonstrates in a scene from Mark's Gospel (6:30-34). First, he tells his exuberant disciples, who are impressed by their own labors, "Come away to a deserted place all by yourselves and rest a while." Later, when he looks out on the vast crowd that has followed them, "he had compassion for them, because they were like sheep without a shepherd." So, Jesus begins to teach them, and later, as the Gospel story continues, to feed them all from a few scraps of ordinary food—a clear Eucharistic reference.

He is our *peace*.

Jesus drives this point home from the cross on which he was nailed. From there, he looks out over his fallen, hungry people with compassion, and cries out, "Father, forgive them; for they do not know what they are doing" (Luke 23:34). And just before he hands over his spirit, he says, "It is finished" (John 19:30). Redemption and reconciliation have been accomplished through his beaten, defeated, (seemingly) destroyed body. Power is made perfect in weakness (cf. 2 Corinthians 12:9).

While chaos still seems to prevail all around us, "all things work together for good for those who love God" (Romans 8:28). New life is breathed into our troubled souls through the blood of the Cross. While the battle threatens to rage on around us and within us, the victory has been won.

*He* is our peace.

While it is always helpful to gaze *upon* the Cross to enter into this mystery, it is also worthwhile to consider another perspective— that of Christ's *from* the cross. What did he see? What was his viewpoint? Can we place ourselves on the cross and see what he saw? Thousands of artists have depicted the crucifixion in various ways, but in the late 19th century, the French painter James Tissot asked these questions, creating the piece titled *What Our Lord Saw from the Cross*. The only parts of Jesus' body visible are his feet at the very bottom. And looking up at him is a sea of humanity whose feet he washes clean with his very own blood.

From this vantage point, he looks out on the world, on you and me, from the beginning to the end of time, and his heart is moved with compassion, for we are like sheep without a shepherd. And he cries out, "Father, forgive them; for they do not know what they are doing."

He is *our* peace. It is finished.

*"Peace be with you. As the Father has sent me, so I send you"* (John 20:21). ♣

# Rejoice Always

❧

"**R**ejoice always."

"Pray without ceasing."

"Give thanks in all circumstances."

"Do not quench the Spirit."

These brief words from St. Paul in the First Letter to the Thessalonians (5:16-19) comprise a commentary of sorts on the whole of Christian life. This is how we are to live.

Why? Because as Isaiah foretold (61:1-2a, 10-11), Jesus Christ has brought good news to the oppressed, healed the brokenhearted, proclaimed liberty to the captives, released the prisoners, and comforted all who mourn (cf. Luke 4:16-21). This he has done in some way—many ways—for each and every one of us as individuals who fit into God's overall plan of redemption and eternal life. We are each oppressed, brokenhearted, captive, imprisoned, or grieved by something in our lives, and it is the Light of Christ who frees us.

So, as Isaiah proclaims (and Mary echoes in Luke 1:46-55):

*I will greatly rejoice in the Lord,*
*    my whole being shall exult in my God;*
*for he has clothed me with garments*
*        of salvation…*
*As the earth brings forth its shoots,*
*    and as a garden causes what is sown in it*
*            to spring up,*
*so the Lord God will cause righteousness*
*        and praise*
*    to spring up before all the nations.*

However, as my confrere Fr. Eugene Hensell, O.S.B., pointed out once in a homily, it is difficult for us to rejoice for any sustained amount of time. It's much easier to be critical, negative, and sorrowful. It is difficult for us to stay focused on the fact that while things in this world are not—and never will be—perfect, from the Christian perspective they are often good enough. Why? Because we are *liberated people* living in a world that is not the be- and end-all. *That* is a cause for rejoicing!

So, Fr. Eugene remarked, we must remember what we *already have* in Christ Jesus, while also looking forward in hope to what is to come.

This doesn't mean, of course, that we go around blissfully ignorant or indifferent, grinning like idiots, singing "Don't worry, be happy." After all, St. Paul saw more than his fair share of hardship. He encountered resistance, conflict, and his own sins. He was beaten, imprisoned, shipwrecked, and eventually martyred. Yet, he tells the Thessalonians (and Philippians) to *rejoice always* as he did.

Why? Because like a lamp, he carried within himself the Light of Christ to help illuminate our dark world from within. He delivered the good news that in Christ, God has clothed each of us with a robe of salvation. As St. Paul says, "The one who calls you is faithful, and he will do this" (1 Thessalonians 5:24).

For this reason and this alone we must rejoice always, pray without ceasing, give thanks in all circumstances, and keep the flame of the Spirit stirred within us. When we each do this—testify to the Light—Christ the Living Flame will come in all his glory to gather all to himself, and our thirst will be eternally satisfied.

In the meantime, as St. Paul writes to the Philippians (4:4-7):

*Rejoice in the Lord always; again I will say, rejoice!*
*Let your gentleness be known to everyone.*
*The Lord is near. Do not worry about anything,*
*but in everything by prayer and supplication*
*with thanksgiving let your requests be made known to God.*
*And the peace of God, which surpasses all understanding,*
*will guard your hearts and minds in Christ Jesus.*

# Joy of the Cross and Resurrection

Lent is a season for intentional reflection, repentance, and renewal. The penitential observances and atmosphere of Lent are meant to remind us that as sinful human beings, we are ultimately dependent on God's mercy and grace. The increased emphasis on prayer, fasting, almsgiving, and other works are designed to "clear away the clutter," so to speak, so we may focus more intently on improving our relationship with God and responding in our daily lives to the grace he provides.

However, lest we become discouraged or too intent on "redeeming ourselves," we also need to recall that as Christians we are a people of the *Resurrection*. The Fourth Sunday of Lent, traditionally referred to as *Laetare* (or Rejoice) Sunday, offers a mid-Lent pause or break from the season's austerity. On *Laetare* Sunday, we are reminded of the entire Paschal Mystery—that Christ not only died for our sins, but rose from the dead, ascended to the Father in Heaven, and sent the Holy Spirit to assist us in following him.

On *Laetare* Sunday, also known as "Rose" or "Refreshment" Sunday, the violet color of vestments and altar cloths are replaced with rose. Churches stripped of flowers for Lent may have them on that Sunday. The Introit for Mass beckons: "Rejoice, Jerusalem!"—referring to Isaiah 66:10-11. In other words, we are provided a foretaste of Easter glory, a refreshing reminder that we are called to be people who live joyfully in the Light of the Resurrection. This is what *every* celebration of the Eucharist is meant to provide: "Do this in memory of me."

Many phrases from Scripture offer comforting words recalling God's immense love for us and the reason for our rejoicing—on *Laetare* Sunday, at Easter, during Lent, or any other season of the year:

> "... *he had compassion on his people... God, who is rich in mercy ... by grace you have been saved... we are what he has made us, created in Christ Jesus for good works, which God prepared beforehand... for God so loved the world... God did not send his Son into the world to condemn the world, but in order that the world might be saved through him... those who do what is true come to the light...*"
>
> (2 Chronicles 36:15; Ephesians 2:4-5, 10; John 3:16-17, 21)

In John 3:14-21, Jesus points to Moses as his precursor, promising eternal life to all who look upon him for salvation. Here, he recalls an Old Testament passage (Numbers 21:4-9), in which Moses mounts a bronze serpent on a pole for the people (who have been bitten by venomous snakes) to look upon and be healed. Likewise, for our sake, God made him (Jesus, God made man) to *be* sin who did not know sin, so that *we* might become the righteousness of God in Christ (cf. 2 Corinthians 5:21).

We look to the Cross, where our sin is nailed in Christ, and beyond it to the Resurrection, where we have been raised with Christ from the dead to live in the Eternal Light of God. Now, *that* is something to *rejoice* about! ♣

# A Moment in Our Hearts

*If you, O Lord, should mark iniquities,*
*Lord, who could stand?*
*But there is forgiveness with you,*
*so that you may be revered.*
—Psalm 130:3-4

God writes straight on the crooked lines of humanity which veer from his will this way and that. And he does so even with supreme foreknowledge of the sometimes violent and disastrous effects our erroneous exercise of free will visits upon humanity, ourselves included.

In the midst of a world filled with such horror, hurt, and hatred—acts of terrorism such as 9/11, school shootings, and yes, abuse committed or allowed by members of the Church—is it possible to even think about forgiveness? Can we even discuss God's mercy? And can the Church—in her flawed existence—still serve as a beacon of hope for the world to see and take refuge in, whether acknowledged as such or not?

Yes. Yes. Yes. Even amid all the violence and pain and hatred still present in the world—even at this precise moment. *Especially* at this moment. As God's people, we need to forgive, to know how to *be* forgiven, and to work for the peace of forgiveness that, by God's grace, radiates out to transform the world.

We see all too clearly what effects hatred, vengeance, and lust for control have on our world. It has been a familiar story for centuries upon centuries. Only the circumstances and their coverage by the evolving media have changed. But be assured, *God will not be thwarted.* He cannot be defeated. In Christ, the victory has already been won— and I am not even *remotely* speaking in military, political, cultural, ideological, or even "religious" terms. This is the truth of a spiritual reality that transcends all else, yet permeates everything in both manifest and hidden ways.

Jesus—God made man—allowed himself to be nailed to a cross by his own misguided creation, and cried out: "Forgive them; for they do not know what they are doing" (Luke 23:34). And before he died on that cross, God-made-man turned to the repentant criminal hanging beside him—someone who never acknowledged him until facing his own death—and said: "Today you will be with me in Paradise" (Luke 23:43).

Three days after his dying on the cross, Jesus rose from the tomb, showing us that God's life conquers death. Then, he ascended into Heaven as both God and man, the only way humanity is capable of entering Paradise.

Be assured that this mercy, this forgiveness *is at work in the world*, at this very moment. It will not be replayed over and over on CNN like the hatred, vengeance, and lust for control will be. But it is there, and it is much more powerful than anything that confronts it or grabs the attention. God takes our broken humanity in all its wickedness and ugliness and redeems it through his very being.

While the world churns and chafes, in the early morning hours here at the monastery, we regularly pray at Vigils through Psalm 68:18-20.

> *You have ascended the high mount,*
>    *leading captives in your train*
>    *and receiving gifts from people,*
> *even from those who rebel against*
>        *the Lord God's abiding there . . .*
> *Blessed be the Lord,*
>    *who daily bears us up;*
>    *God is our salvation.*
> *Our God is a God of salvation,*
>    *and to God, the Lord, belongs escape*
>        *from death.*

Who has *rebelled*? Each and every one of us. Yet God's mercy, his redemptive grace, is extended to each one of us. But it isn't something we can just take for ourselves. It is a gift we share—the gift that keeps on giving, as the saying goes. There is hope, there is peace for those who embrace this and believe in it, despite any seeming evidence to the contrary. Jesus did not come to fight humanity, to condemn the world, but to save the misguided creation he loves without end (cf. John 3:16-17).

There is an infinite amount of peace in that if it is reflected upon long enough. And that divine peace from on high *is* in the world, small but growing, like the mustard seed or the yeast in the rising dough that Jesus compared with the Kingdom of God (cf. Matthew 13:31-33 and Luke 13:18-21). Basically, we have two choices—either to consume and become that mustard seed, that yeast of mercy, *in our daily lives*, or to cling to our wrath, which ultimately consumes and overtakes us individually and collectively.

As the Book of Sirach says: "Anger and wrath, these also are abominations, yet a sinner holds on to them." (27:30-28:7). The one who cherishes wrath will die in it because he or she has refused the gift of mercy which God freely offers to all.

Yes, mercy is a gift with a personal price, but one that pays innumerable dividends for all. It is not easy, and it is not quick. *But it is the only thing in this world that truly heals.* When we forgive, we receive forgiveness, all through the God of Mercy. Jesus is quite clear with his parable of the unforgiving servant in Matthew's Gospel (18:21-35) and also with his teachings on prayer: "Our Father. . . . forgive us our trespasses *as we forgive* those who trespass against *us*" (cf. Matthew 6:7-15; Mark 11:25; Luke 11:1-4). When we do this, we cry out with Jesus from the cross, "Forgive them; for they do not know what they are doing."

This is not some vague, over-arching effort directed toward the world at large. It *starts in the heart*, within the particular circumstances and relationships of our daily lives and radiates out from that. Peace does not enter our hearts from the world. *Peace enters the world from within our hearts.*

It starts with that small mustard seed, that bit of yeast, God-made-man as an infant in a stable manger. And it works slowly but surely, rising and converging into the Bread of Life.

Healing is not instant. The scars we inflict upon ourselves in myriad ways are still there, and they often run very deep. But as Fr. Carroll Stuhlmueller, C.P., once observed:

> Even the healthiest of human bodies needs time to recover from sickness and be totally healed. While the act of forgiveness takes only a moment, the full effects cover a longer sweep of time and require careful attention . . . Forgiveness, too, involves a process.

But it is a process that *begins* with a moment—a moment in our hearts. ♣

# Redemption and Resurrection

# Flowering—from the Ground Up

S pring always arrives early in southern Indiana—or so it seems to someone who, before coming to the monastery, spent 40-plus years living primarily in northern Ohio. In that region, winter usually lingers long past its welcome.

In any event, whatever time spring arrives, it is *always* welcome. Trees unfolding their fresh ensembles of leaves. Daytime temperatures sometimes stretching into the 70s and even 80s. Emerald carpets of fresh grass. Colorful blossoms everywhere, offering varying hues of hope for the once-dreary landscape and the often weary soul.

Hope indeed springs eternal.

What does this hope, this blossoming, spring *from*? Seemingly, it arises from lifelessness, which is why the season gives us an extra *spring* in our step. Everything is new and promising again. What was dead (or seemed so) has come back to life. A tiny seed planted many months ago in the dark, cold earth has decayed and fallen apart—to reveal a green sprout, then a stalk, and eventually branches, blossoms, and fruit held high above the ground. Whether spring is early or late, this happens every year. I always marvel at that.

The very tangible effects of this mystery beckon us to recall an even greater one—the flowering of eternal salvation for all of humanity from what was dead (or seemed so). In John's Gospel (12:20-33), Jesus uses very tangible terms and familiar images to draw us into this mystery:

*"Unless a grain of wheat falls into the earth and dies, it remains just a single grain; but if it dies, it bears much fruit. Those who love their life lose it, and those who hate their life in this world will keep it for eternal life. Whoever serves me must follow me."*

With these words, of course, Jesus is indicating his approaching death and resurrection, by which he gives all baptized Christians life. However, he is doing much more than that. He is calling us to follow him in the same manner. He is not telling us to loathe our existence and abhor the world in which we live. Rather, he calls us to *give new life* to the world by dying to ourselves—to our prejudices and preconceived notions, our selfishness, pride, greed, lust, anger, desire to control and consume. For instance, am I holding a grudge against someone? Jesus calls me to sink it into the ground, bury it like a seed, pray for the heavenly dew of mercy, fertilize it by extending forgiveness, and prune myself for reconciliation. Sooner or later, the Light of the Resurrected Christ will bring what was dead back to life, raise up a shoot, an olive branch of peace which bears fruit for many.

Through the death of one tiny such seed, life springs forth. Eternal salvation buds from what had seemed dark, hopeless, and lost.

Like all growing seasons, this is a gradual process requiring many laborers in the field. At the beginning of the passage from John's Gospel cited above, some Greeks (foreigners, not Jews, not the "chosen ones") approach the Apostle Philip (who speaks their language) and say, "We wish to see Jesus." In other words: "We, too, want to believe. Show us how." Philip tells Andrew, and both tell Jesus. The Greeks—like all believers—needed help in coming to the Light, and it didn't happen all at once.

Viewed from this perspective, Jesus' "grain of wheat" analogy takes on universal significance. "It is for this reason that I have come to this hour," Jesus says—the hour of his Passion, Death, Resurrection, and Ascension into Heaven. "When I am lifted up from the earth, I will draw all people to myself."

All people means *all people.* But each person must allow himself or herself to be drawn up with Jesus—to accept the seed of faith planted in our hearts, and to cultivate and care for it in our everyday lives. Then, in due season, we can watch it spring to life and breathe deeply of the fragrance from its blossoms. ♠

# Come Out!

Three relatively short lines in the story of Jesus' raising of Lazarus from the dead (John 11:1-45) summarize and inspire our entire Christian life of faith. One is a proclamation by Jesus. The second is an act of Jesus. The third is an overwhelming display of Jesus' power and compassion as the Son of God. The three lines are:

*"I am the resurrection and the life."*
*Jesus began to weep.*
*"Lazarus, come out!"*

Together, these lines contain a profound promise. Just as with the man born blind in John 9:1-41 and the Samaritan woman at the well in John 4:5-42, Jesus' friend Lazarus represents all of humanity. We are spiritually parched, unseeing, and dead. However, Jesus comes to meet us where we are—the well of shame, the darkness of doubt, and the tomb of isolation. He stands ready to relieve our thirst, give us sight, and bring us out of the depths of loneliness. He wants to liberate us from sin and death, and has the power to do so. As God tells the prophet Ezekiel: "I, the Lord, have spoken and will act" (37:12-14).

How, precisely?

Let us look again at the three lines above from John's Gospel. In the first, Jesus proclaims that the Life of the Resurrection is not just a doctrine or a theory. It is a *person*—God himself made flesh. What Jesus proclaims here, he will *do* as the Paschal Mystery builds during Holy Week and climaxes on Easter Sunday. He *is* the Resurrection and the Life.

In the second line, Jesus demonstrates his human solidarity with us. He shares our sorrows, our pain, and our death amid persistent doubt and confusion—but not only to console us. He weeps with us to embrace our human condition in a manner that promises us eternal life if only we die with his Spirit dwelling in us (cf. Romans 8:8-11).

And in the final line, Jesus conquers death, the wage of sin (cf. Romans 6:23), in ordering out of the tomb a dead man—who obeys! Ironically, this action will ultimately lead to his own death, but in a double-twist of irony, Lazarus' rising prefigures the resurrection of Jesus—*and ours with him*. God has the last word.

As you meditate on this beautiful passage from John's Gospel, picture yourself as Lazarus in the tomb, bound in the burial cloths of sin and death. Imagine the stone being rolled away, light creeping in, and hearing Jesus' voice outside calling to you:

*"Come out!"*

You are untied, freed.

Do you believe this? ♠

# Ashes to Ashes

*"You are dust,*
*and to dust you shall return."*
—Genesis 3:19

I n his *Rule* for monks, St. Benedict writes that one must "keep death daily before your eyes" (*Rule* 4:47). The tomb, just as it received Christ's lifeless body on Good Friday, awaits each and every one of us.

This is not a macabre admonition or an invitation to be perpetually morose. Quite the opposite, as the preceding sentence in the passage from the *Rule* demonstrates: "Yearn for everlasting life with holy desire." Like the ancient Israelites, we are sojourners under the watchful and protecting gaze of our compassionate God as we travel to the Promised Land of eternal life through the love of Christ.

Our annual observance of Lent is a reminder that the world as we know it is not the be-all and end-all. Something—or, more precisely, *Someone*—infinitely better awaits us. The joy of this knowledge, derived through faith, fills us with that holy desire needed to live radically here and now so that, as St. Benedict says toward the end of his *Rule*, Christ may bring us all together to everlasting life.

This is the hope that fills our days with joy without denying our deep sorrow. It is what makes us Christian. When things go terribly wrong, when failure and hardship seem to frame our days, and when people age and die, what we are really lamenting is the brokenness of Creation. We *should* feel sorrow, because the life for which God created us was not meant to be that way. However, we should *also* embrace the joy of knowing that in Christ, God has restored all things, and rightly ordered them as they are meant to be.

It is true that from our limited perspective, we cannot fully perceive that right-ordering. In Christ, however, the act has been completed, but is still growing to fulfillment. Similarly, when we plant a flower bulb in the earth during the lengthening shadows of autumn, we know that it will be months before it springs forth from the ground with life and color and fragrance—but its work has begun. The Incarnation continues to this very moment as the Body of Christ grows to maturity in each one of us. Truly, "with the Lord one day is like a thousand years, and a thousand years are like one day" (2 Peter 3:8).

The moment has been redeemed, and eternity calls out to us from the dark moments just before the dawn. Listen, and from the silence of the tomb, cling to Jesus' words to his disciples the night before he died:

*"Do not let your hearts be troubled. Believe in God, believe also in me. In my Father's house there are many dwelling places. If I go and prepare a place for you, I will come again and will take you to myself, so that where I am, there you may be also. You know the way to the place where I am going . . . I am the way, and the truth, and the life"*

—John 14:1-4, 6

# Children of the Resurrection

Some translations of a passage from Luke's Gospel interpret the phrase "the ones who will rise" as "children of the resurrection" (20:36). What a wonderful promise!

While it is quite common today—and through many previous ages—to believe in life after death, it is often conceived of as a *spiritual* resurrection only, even among many Christians. This is a mistaken notion, and not what the Church teaches. What Scripture and tradition make clear is that ours will also be a *bodily* resurrection (cf. 2 Maccabees 7:1-2, 9-14; Luke 24:36-43; John 20:19-29; Romans 8:10-11, 22-23; 1 Corinthians 15).

One needs to look no further than the resurrection of Christ himself. Jesus was raised from the dead with his own body—albeit one that was spiritually transformed and glorified. Fully divine, *and* fully human, he announces to us: "I am the resurrection and the life" (John 11:25). Those who receive him also receive the promise of his resurrection on the Last Day. ❦

# Little Fishes of Christ

Fish (along with bread) are mentioned frequently in the gospels and are typically associated with Christ in a Eucharistic context. All four gospels contain various accounts of the multiplication of loaves and fish by Jesus—twice in Mark and Matthew, and once in Luke and John. Fish are also eaten by Jesus and his disciples in the post-resurrection appearances recounted at the end of Luke and John. Not coincidentally, several of the apostles were fishermen, to whom Jesus called, "I will make you fish for people" (Matthew 4:19).

So it is no surprise that the fish became a primary symbol for the early Christians, who apparently used it from the beginning, particularly in artwork and funerary slabs, until the time of Constantine, according to the *Encyclopedia of the Early Church*. "It almost always clearly represents Christ, though sometimes standing for the Christian, and its history can be traced from its appearance in the [early] second century down to the fourth, when it begins gradually to disappear on Christian monuments," writes C.R. Morey in a 1910 article in the *Princeton Theological Review*.

The symbol of the fish represented Christ, and signified not only the Eucharist, but Baptism, the Last Supper, the Resurrection, and eternal life, and "as the cross denoted the ever-present danger of persecution until the middle of the fourth century, the fish identified individuals as Christians," writes Diane Apostolos-Cappadonia in the *Dictionary of Christian Art*.

In this light, its popularity among the early Christians, who sometimes needed to be careful about how they identified themselves, is due to the acrostic formed by the ancient Greek word for fish, *ichthys*. The word is formed with the initial letters of the five Greek words for "Jesus Christ, Son of God, Savior" (*Iesous Christos Theou Yios Soter*) and the acrostic is recognized as "IXΘYC." As such, the acrostic, or the image of a fish, or both, comprised a profession of faith in the divinity of Christ, the Redeemer of mankind, states *The Catholic Encyclopedia.*

Believers, then, became "little fishes," sharing in Christ's baptism and resurrection through the Eucharist. Just as a fish cannot live out of water, the Christian cannot live outside of Christ. These images are often combined in writings of the early fathers, and particularly in artwork and inscriptions contained within the Roman catacombs.

One of the most famous examples of this is from the early Christian writer Tertullian (b. 150), who in his treatise *On Baptism* wrote: "We little fishes are born in water, after the example of our *Ichthys* Jesus Christ. And we have safety in no other way than by permanently abiding in water."

This type of representation also appears in the ancient epitaph of Abercius, a second-century bishop of Hierapolis in Phrygia, which Joannes Quasten, in his four-volume work *Patrology*, calls "the queen of all ancient Christian inscriptions." Written in a metaphorical, mystical style common to its day, it is a good text for meditation in any age. In part it reads:

> *Everywhere faith led the way*
> *and set before me for food the fish from the spring,*
> *mighty and pure, whom a spotless Virgin caught,*
> *and gave this to friends to eat, always*
> *having sweet wine and giving the mixed cup with bread.*

This is the oldest monument of stone mentioning the Eucharist, and as Quasten explains, Abercius is describing a journey on which he shared the Eucharist with fellow Christians: "The fish from the spring, mighty and pure, is Christ, according to the acrostic IXΘYC. The spotless Virgin who caught the fish is, according to the language of the time, the Virgin Mary, who conceived the Savior."

May all "little fishes" share in this feast!

Precisely how this happens is a mystery, but the real question for us to ponder is this: If Jesus' Resurrection embraces our humanity, then how does our humanity embrace his Resurrection? In other words, how are you living the Resurrection *today*, with the body and soul given you by God?

We are God's children *now* (1 John 3:2), children of the Resurrection! May the Lord direct our hearts toward this promise. ♣

# What Then Should We Do?

How in the world is a Christian supposed to rejoice in times like these—so full of suffering, evil, death? How can we believe in a promise of redemption from a loving, merciful God, considering all the harm and horror that so many people experience?

There's no getting around the pain and sorrow, for example, of school shootings, when calculated rage extinguishes barely budding futures and inflicts nightmarish wounds among survivors, relatives, and friends which will echo for a lifetime. Such unspeakable massacres grab our attention because they are so concentrated into one time and place. But other horrors abound worldwide each day—almost at every moment. The slaughter of civil war continues. Violent unrest and repression persist. Famine, pestilence, and scarcity of such necessities as water and medicine are the only realities generations of people in many under-developed regions have ever known.

Outwardly, this country enjoys relative peace and ease. Inwardly, though, it is at war. Addiction, sexual abuse, racism, and pure greed afflict untold thousands. Senseless violence, suicide, traffic accidents, cancer, and chronic illness wreak havoc with our lives. Homelessness, mental illness, unemployment, and poverty plague more people in this land of prosperity than we care to acknowledge. There is corruption and scandal. Spouses cheat on one another. Too many live by the adage, "If it feels good, do it," while others suffer from despair, doubt, and loneliness.

*Not fair. Why?*

Right. I don't know. Nobody does. None of it is God's will (cf. Ezekiel 18:32).

Yet, for some reason which we cannot begin to comprehend, God *does allow it* to occur. He respects our freedom of will enough to allow us to dwell, so to speak, in the muck we ourselves create (individually and collectively). All the while, many point fingers at one another and even blame the God some say doesn't exist because he would never allow such horrors!

It's an age-old pattern that humanity keeps repeating (cf. Genesis 3:12-13). Scripture itself is not immune. The Old Testament is bathed in blood. It is filled with the same sort of human ugliness we encounter today. We can't help ourselves, and neither could those who came before us. It's a wonder we're allowed to exist at all—except that deep down, we know that in the beginning, we were created in the image of God, who is Love.

So, something is *obviously* off.

Through it all, God beckons us through the voices of prophet after prophet, in effect saying, "My beloved children, have you had enough yet? Please, stop it. Turn back. Come to me. I will heal you, comfort you, forgive you, give you more than you can ask or imagine. Take my hand and come. I will lead you, though you cannot see. Do not be afraid. Trust me. Come to the feast."

Few listen. One after another, prophets are killed for their words of wisdom. Finally, in the person of Jesus, God himself comes among us. He inserts himself into the midst of the ugliness like a commando penetrating the enemy's defenses to attack from within. He injects peace into the heart of war. He teaches. He works miracles. He leads.

And we kill him, too. But he's clever. He really dies, but he comes back—is resurrected (he told us he would, but we weren't listening). God himself became sin, sucking up into himself all that pus oozing from disfigured humanity. Then, he allowed it to be destroyed forever in his body on a cross, so that like him, we might rise to new and eternal life, cleansed and transformed. Death is defeated. We are restored as children of God. What we can't do for ourselves, God does for us.

That's what they say, anyway. Thousands have taught that message, and suffered and died for it when they could just as easily have walked away and lived in relative ease. So, there must be something to it.

*But the world is still a rotten place.*

Yes, in some ways, perhaps.

*Nothing's really changed.*

Hasn't it? Do we see, know, understand *everything* that is, and will be—really?

*What are we supposed to do, just ignore all the suffering and think happy thoughts all the time?*

Of course not. That would be inhuman. As St. Paul says elsewhere, we must "weep with those who weep" (Romans 12:15). And so we do. It is only right. And still, at this very moment, God's goodness pours out in myriad ways upon those who are afflicted. For example, God's goodness worked through those who consoled the people of Newtown, Connecticut (where 28 people, most of them young children, were massacred by a lone gunman in December 2012). God's goodness was present in those teachers and administrators who risked and/or lost their lives for the sake of their students.

*But why does it seem to take something so horrific to occur, so many innocent people to suffer, before that goodness is exhibited?*

Good question. I suspect that most of the time, it's there, quietly working, but it often flies underneath our radar until something tragic heightens our senses. God is present among us every day in innumerable ways. We must look for the good, even amid the horrendous, and trust that somehow, he's straightening out what we have made crooked.

*But if death was defeated forever on the cross, why do the innocent still suffer? Why doesn't God just put an end to it?*

Another good question. Perhaps the 11th chapter of John's Gospel holds some clues. Jesus' good friend Lazarus is sick. Although he works miracles for many others whom he barely knows, Jesus does nothing. Lazarus dies. Jesus travels to meet Lazarus' family and friends. The mourners, including Lazarus' sisters Mary and Martha, ask Jesus in effect, "Why didn't you do anything?"

Then we are hit with possibly the most powerful words in all of Scripture: "Jesus began to weep" (John 11:35). He mourns with those who mourn. God suffers *with* us.

Then, he does something amazing—he raises Lazarus back to life. All this is meant to foreshadow Jesus' own death, and by extension, each of ours. Shortly thereafter, Jesus is crucified while people around him say, "Save yourself! Why don't you do anything?" Jesus cries out, "Father, forgive them; for they do not know what they are doing," (Luke 23:34). God's mercy descends on the undeserving, and three days later, there is an astonishing exclamation point: his Resurrection, and by extension, the promise of resurrection for each of us.

It is beyond our comprehension: God allows unspeakable evil and brings about unimaginable good. In the end, we are told, all will be ordered as it should be, as it was meant to be from the beginning, through the Alpha and the Omega (cf. Revelation 21:1-7).

*So, everybody's "off the hook"?*

Not by a long shot. Christ crucified gives meaning to what otherwise is pure madness, decay, and death. As the French poet Paul Claudel said, "Jesus did not come to remove suffering, or to explain it, but to fill it with his presence." He became *part* of our suffering, *part* of humanity's story, in order to redeem it from within, and thereby *involve us* in his divine work of redemption. "When I am lifted up from the earth, I will draw all people to myself," Jesus said (John 12:32).

So, this is our story, too. It is the whole point of the Incarnation. As his disciples, we are called to make Christ present in the world through Word, Sacrament, and the example of a holy life, and to trust that *somehow*, God is redeeming the moment in a manner we can't fully recognize or comprehend. That is our faith, though we are not always faithful.

Like the crowds in Luke's Gospel addressing John the Baptist before the arrival of Jesus, we may then ask: *What then should we do?* (3:10-18).

What does John the Baptist say in this passage? Share your food and clothing with those who have none. Be honest. Put away all greed, extortion, and treachery.

In addition, the Ten Commandments in the Old Testament tell us: Love the Lord your God above all else. Revere him. Worship him. Honor your parents. Do not kill. Do not commit adultery. Do not steal. Do not bear false witness. Do not covet anyone or anything (Exodus 20:2-17).

In the New Testament, Jesus tells us that the blessed include those who are poor in spirit, mourning, meek, those who hunger and thirst for righteousness, the merciful, the clean of heart, the peacemakers, and those persecuted for the sake of righteousness (Matthew 5:3-10).

To sum it all up, Jesus says simply:

> *"You shall love the Lord your God with all your heart, and with all your soul, and with all your mind. And you shall love your neighbor as yourself. Love one another. Just as I have loved you, you also should love one another. By this everyone will know that you are my disciples, if you have love for one another."*
>
> (Matthew 22:37, 39; John 13:34-35)

Because it is humanly impossible for us to do this all the time, he died for us on the cross in loving self-sacrifice. But *because* he died for us on the cross, we must strive to do as he commands. Apart from him, it is true that we can do nothing (cf. John 15:5). But all things are possible for God (cf. Matthew 19:26). It is a work he begins and ends—but by the grace of God, it is one we *participate in* as the Body of Christ.

And so, as that Body, we pray together during Mass the words Jesus taught us to pray:

> *Our Father, who art in heaven,*
> *hallowed be thy name.*
> *Thy Kingdom come, thy will be done*
> *on earth as it is in heaven.*
> *Give us this day our daily bread,*
> *and forgive us our trespasses,*
> *as we forgive those who trespass against us;*
> *and lead us not into temptation,*
> *but deliver us from evil.*

Moments later, we sing together, "Lamb of God, you take away the sins of the world, have mercy on us/grant us peace," while the consecrated bread is snapped and broken into many pieces to be shared and consumed by each one of us. In all of us, those many pieces constitute the *one* Body of Christ, and so we are sent out: "Go in peace, glorifying the Lord by your life."

Though we must still live with our wounded nature—our clay jars—we carry forth the treasure we have received in Christ "so that it may be made clear that this extraordinary power belongs to God and does not come from us. We are afflicted in every way, but not crushed; perplexed, but not driven to despair; persecuted, but not forsaken; struck down, but not destroyed; always carrying in the body the death of Jesus, so that the life of Jesus may also be made visible in our bodies" (2 Corinthians 4:7-10).

Because of this, we rejoice, on this day and every day, even in times like these—*especially in times like these*, even as we weep with those who weep. Together, "we await the blessed hope and the coming of our Savior, Jesus Christ," who is with us always, until the end of the age (cf. Matthew 28:20). As St. Paul (who, incidentally, was writing from prison) says in Philippians 4:4-7:

> *"Rejoice in the Lord always; again I will say, Rejoice! Let your gentleness be known to everyone. The Lord is near. Do not worry about anything, but in everything by prayer and supplication with thanksgiving let your requests be made known to God. And the peace of God, which surpasses all understanding, will guard your hearts and your minds in Christ Jesus. Finally, beloved, whatever is true, whatever is honorable, whatever is just, whatever is pure, whatever is pleasing, whatever is commendable, if there is any excellence and if there is anything worthy of praise, think about these things."*

Christians rejoice because while time is still unfolding the history of salvation, the moment has been redeemed in eternity. We rejoice because we believe that throughout it all, the holy innocents dance with delight around the Christ child. In harmony, these "eternal imitations" of Christ (Charles Peguy) rejoice in the hope that is stored up in Heaven for all of us. ♣

# The Joy of the Banquet

E aster Sunday, the Day of the Resurrection, calls us to enter more fully into the mystery of the overwhelming, unmerited, totally gratuitous, and life-changing gift of grace that God is always extending to us. This is the central theme of Scripture and our faith tradition: God offers us an eternal share in the divine life—beginning *right now*, no matter what season it is. Out of love, God desires to lavish upon us his goodness, imploring: "Come to the wedding banquet" (Matthew 22:4).

However, we often refuse the invitation. Throughout most of history, human beings (particularly in the West) have clung to the notion that "there's no such thing as a free lunch." We don't understand unmerited, totally gratuitous grace (or any gift that meets such criteria, it seems). We fear what we think it might demand of us. Sure, the "meal" may be great, but when the bill arrives—look out! Perhaps that's why we so often hesitate or refuse God's perpetual invitation of grace.

We are much more comfortable with paying the price of admission, earning our keep, or climbing the ladder of success (even if it means stepping over—or on—others in the process). We don't know how to accept a free gift. We'd rather earn it—or repay it with an even greater gift, so we can come out on top in the equation. *That,* we understand. We need to be worthy, and if we can't, then at least we're not going to be outdone.

But when it comes to our relationship with God, the fact is that we *are* outdone—and always will be. We can never "measure up" or achieve God's favor. *And the good news is that we don't have to!* God still says, "Come to the banquet." No payment is required; none will be accepted. The only thing we need to do is recognize and accept God's invitation, and then enjoy the banquet of grace. In such a state of communion, only *then* will we be impelled to extend God's graciousness to others through good works—not as repayment, but as a humble gesture of gratitude and the desire to share our joy with others who have not yet tasted and seen that the Lord is good (cf. Psalm 34:8). Grace is a gift to be given away—only to be replenished in even greater measure.

This theme of grace is woven throughout the entire Bible. For example, it is signified by the manna God rained down on the ancient Israelites in the desert despite their grumpy waywardness (as told in the Book of Exodus). Later, the True Bread from Heaven (cf. John 6:32) shared common meals with a multitude of people—particularly those labeled as being unworthy sinners and outcasts. Then, at the Last Supper, he gathered his still uncomprehending and imperfect disciples, took the bread and wine, blessed it, broke it, and shared it with them, saying "Do this in remembrance of me" (cf. Luke 22:14-20).

Finally, as a profound exclamation point, this Jesus, who so often spoke of festive banquets as a symbol for the Kingdom of God, offered his life to the Father on the cross to demonstrate the gratuitous nature of the eternal banquet. He paid the price, once and for all, to open the door of the banquet hall—not *after* we demonstrate that we are good enough to enter, but while we are *still sinners* (cf. Romans 5:8). As Richard Rohr has written, "God does not love you because you are good. God loves you because God is good."

Perfection is not required—only authentic humility and faith. And this applies *today*—not merely in some distant time and place. *Today* God "prepares a banquet" for us (cf. Isaiah 49:8; 2 Corinthians 6:2; Psalm 23:5), holding out to us more abundance than we can possibly imagine.

God is merciful, compassionate, loving, faithful, and gracious. He loves to throw a party and wants us all there—now and forever. And he spares no expense:

> *"Everyone who thirsts, come to the waters; and you that have no money, come, buy and eat! Come, buy wine and milk without money and with-*

*out price. Why do you spend your money for that which is not bread, and your labor for that which does not satisfy? Listen carefully to me, and eat what is good, and delight yourselves in rich food."*

—Isaiah 55:1-2

Let us not fear the invitation, be distracted from it, ignore it, or misinterpret the entire message as another method of calculating payment. Let us recall that three days after he died on the cross, the single grain of wheat planted in the tomb rose as the Bread of Life and fills our nostrils with the delightful scent of the Holy Spirit (cf. John 20:22).

The joy of the banquet is ours (cf. John 15:11). All we must do is accept it and choose to be transformed by the Risen Life of Christ. All are welcome. Admission is free. Taste and see. The Lord is good. ♣

"The Lord sustained his people in a desert land,
    In a howling wilderness waste;
He shielded them, cared for them,
    guarded them as the apple of his eye.
As an eagle stirs up its nest,
    and hovers over its young;
as it spreads its wings, takes them up,
    and bears them aloft on its pinions,
the Lord alone guided them."
                                —Deuteronomy 32:10-12

225

# *Liturgical Year Index*

Most of the scriptural reflections compiled in this book are adapted from posts on my personal blog (first, *yokeofchrist.blogspot.com*, and, later, *pathoflifeblog.blogspot.com*) from 2009 to 2013. Although most were originally written with a view toward the liturgical year in the Roman Catholic Church and its Sunday cycle of readings for Mass, they were adapted and arranged thematically in this book. For those interested in reading the reflections in view of their original correspondence with the three-year liturgical cycle of Sunday readings, this index is provided (there are not reflections for every day of the liturgical year in all three cycles).

**PLEASE NOTE**: *not every reflection in the book is listed in this index, since several were originally written without any reference to a specific point in the liturgical year. Also, in cases where the Mass readings for a certain feast or solemnity are the same regardless of liturgical cycle (Year A, B, or C), the corresponding reflection is listed under the heading Solemnities and Feasts; otherwise, each is listed under the appropriate year from the liturgical cycle.*

—Br. Francis

## <u>Year A</u>

### Advent/Christmas

# Liturgical Index

# Liturgical Index

# Liturgical Index

# *Liturgical Index*

# Liturgical Index

# Liturgical Index

## Year C

### Advent/Christmas

Third Sunday of Advent
(Zephaniah 3:14-18a; Philippians 4:4-7; Luke 3:10-18)
— *What Then Should We Do?*, 216

### Ordinary Time

Twenty-eighth Sunday
(2 Kings 5:14-17; 2 Timothy 2:8-13; Luke 17:11-19)
— *Remember*, 143

Thirtieth Sunday
(Sirach 35:12-14, 16-18; 2 Timothy 4:6-8, 16-18; Luke 18:9-14)
— *Piercing the Clouds*, 112

Thirty-first Sunday
(Wisdom 11:22—12:2; 2 Thessalonians 1:11—2:2; Luke 19:1-10)
— *Lover of Souls*, 171

Thirty-second Sunday
(2 Maccabees 7:1-2, 9-14; 2 Thessalonians 2:16—3:5;
Luke 20:27-38)
— *Children of the Resurrection*, 213

### Lent/Easter

First Sunday of Lent
(Deuteronomy 26:4-10; Romans 10:8-13; Luke 4:1-13)
— *Choosing the Wise Path*, 130

## Solemnities and Feasts

*When Mass readings are the same for years A, B, C*

Solemnity of the Nativity of the Lord,
(Christmas, Mass during the Night)
(Isaiah 9:1-6; Titus 2:11-14; Luke 2:1-14)
— *Light Shines in the Darkness*, 149

Feast of the Holy Innocents, December 28
(1 John 1:5—2:2; Matthew 2:13-18)
— *Small Wonder*, 93

# *Liturgical Index*

## MISCELLANEOUS

# About the Author

**Br. Francis Wagner, O.S.B.**, is a Benedictine monk of Saint Meinrad Archabbey in St. Meinrad, Indiana, and is an editor and writer for Path of Life Publications at the Abbey Press. The author of several publications and articles in the fields of spirituality and pastoral care, he is also a conference presenter for the Benedictine oblate program and serves as a spiritual director.

## Section Photograph Descriptions

Grace: *Subiaco, Italy, 2010*

Prayer: *Ludesch, Austria, 2010*

The Body of Christ: *Annecy, France, 2010*

Conversion: *St. Meinrad, Indiana, 2010*

God in the Moment: *St. Meinrad, Indiana, 2010*

Christian Life: *Ufenau Island, Switzerland, 2010*

Faith: *Zermatt, Switzerland, 2010*

Hope: *St. Meinrad, Indiana, 2012*

Love: *Little Matterhorn, Switzerland, 2010*

Peace and Joy: *St. Meinrad, Indiana, 2011*

Redemption and Resurrection: *St. Meinrad, Indiana, 2011*